YESHIVAH GEDOL/

735 Avenue C • Bayonne, New Je

With the rapid growth of dynamic Torah Jewry in America, we have seen a new proliferation of *yeshivos* over the last decade to serve the rising need. Among the forefront of these *yeshivos* is the Yeshivah Gedolah of Bayonne. In the short few years since its establishment in 1990, it has already become one of the *yeshivos* of first choice, with applications far outstripping capacity. Located in Bayonne, New Jersey, it draws its student body not only from the metropolitan area of Greater New York but from as far away as Boston, Detroit and Los Angeles.

The Yeshivah Gedolah of Bayonne offers a singular blend of personal attention, academic excellence and nurturing of good *midos* and *yiras shamayim*. The method of study puts a major emphasis on *lomdus*, the analytic system of Talmud study, following in the traditions of such Torah giants as Rav Aharon Kotler, Rav Leib Malin and Rav Berel Soloveitchik, who had a major influence on the growth of Torah in America and Eretz Yisrael during the postwar period. There is a also a very warm and mutually beneficent relationship with the local community, which the presence of the *yeshivah* has dramatically revitalized.

The Yeshivah Gedolah of Bayonne has been able to accomplish so much in such relatively little time, because it is very rich in human resources, with a very talented and dedicated staff and administration. Unfortunately, however, we are not so rich in financial resources, and with the rapid growth of the *yeshivah*, the financial burden is becoming increasing more difficult to carry. Therefore, we must reach out to our friends and supporters to help us continue our important work. Only through such a partnership can the bright promising future of the *yeshivah* be fulfilled.

JEWISH
Glimpses of
FRANKFURT

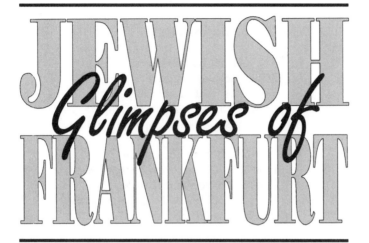

JEWISH Glimpses of FRANKFURT

BY RABBI Y. ALFASI

translated and edited by

RABBI AVRAHAM YAAKOV FINKEL

CIS

P·U·B·L·I·S·H·E·R·S

New York · London · Jerusalem

Published and distributed
in the U.S., Canada and overseas by
C.I.S. Publishers and Distributors
180 Park Avenue, Lakewood, New Jersey 08701
(908) 905-3000 Fax: (908) 367-6666

Distributed in Israel by
C.I.S. International (Israel)
Rechov Mishkalov 18
Har Nof, Jerusalem
Tel: 02-518-935

Distributed in the U.K. and Europe by
C.I.S. International (U.K.)
89 Craven Park Road
London N15 6AH, England
Tel: 81-809-3723

Book and cover design: Deenee Cohen
Typography: Chaya Bleier

Library of Congress Catalog Number
93-072492

ISBN 1-56062-213-X hard cover
1-56062-214-8 soft cover

PRINTED IN THE UNITED STATES OF AMERICA

Glimpses of JEWISH FRANKFURT

Table of Contents

List of Photographs

Publisher's Note

One of the great strengths of the Jewish people has always been their superlative sense of community, of caring for each other and relying on each other, of commonly shared joys and sorrows, of each individual being a component of a much larger social organism, the whole of which is much greater than the sum of its parts. Two thousand years ago, when the bulk of the Jewish people still lived in the relatively small geographic area of Eretz Yisrael, unified by the *Beis Hamikdash*, *Sanhedrin* and shared political, cultural and social conditions, the significance of the *kehillah*, the local community, was relatively minor. But even then, the flourishing communities in Iraq, Egypt and the European centers of the Roman Empire already foreshadowed a divergent development among widely scattered locales.

With the destruction of the *Beis Hamikdash* and the subsequent Diaspora, this became the common experience of all the Jewish people. From that time on, the Jewish communities were no longer guided by a central Torah authority. Their customs, methods of study and applications of the Law to new circumstances began to differ widely according to geographic location. Instead of sharing one history, they were now swept along by the peculiar political, social and economic conditions that affected their respective host countries. And although the basic elements of the Torah and the Talmud remained amazingly resilient and inviolate, geography began to play a predominant role in the character and form of Jewish life.

In the broadest sense, the Sephardic Jews of the Middle East and North Africa differed greatly from the Ashkenazic Jews living in Europe. In a narrower sense, the Jews of Western Europe differed from the Jews of Eastern Europe, the Jews of Lithuania differed from the Jews of Poland, the *chassidim* differed from the *misnagdim*— although they all shared more features with each other than they did with Sephardic Jews. In an even narrower sense, the Jews of one city differed from the Jews of another city, so that the character of Jewish life in Warsaw, for instance, differed from the character of Jewish life in Cracow. Similar subdivisions, of course, developed in the Sephardic world.

The underlying structure of Jewish society became the *kehillah*, and while the wisdom and leadership of universally revered Torah sages were widely accepted and heeded, the functional social unit was the independent local community, and the personalities and leadership qualities of the local rabbis and *parnassim* (lay leaders) often had a more profound impact. Even such temporary regional organizations as the Vaad Arba Haaratzos (the Council of the Four Lands), which governed Polish Jewry from the sixteenth through the eighteenth centuries, only dealt with broader issues and did not submerge the independence of the *kehillah*.

As a result of these new conditions, and over the course

of many centuries, Torah-true Jewish life assumed myriad external forms, each founded on the rock-solid twin foundations of the Written Law and the Oral Law, becoming a veritable *kesoness passim*, a single "coat of many colors." The cultural traits, historical experience and religious and social customs of every single Jewish community in the world are holy and precious, and while each Jew must follow the particular customs and practices of his family tradition, the endless multi-hued variations are all integral parts of our priceless common heritage.

Recent history, however, has taken a different direction. In the aftermath of the holocaust, many of the renowned communities have simply ceased to exist, and their invaluable legacies are in danger of being lost. And even among the survivors, the system of numerous independent, geographically distinct *kehillos* has gone into decline, to be replaced by a system of megacommunities which tend to blend and homogenize their various components.

With this in mind, C.I.S. Publishers feels honored and privileged to launch this new series of short historical sketches of illustrious Jewish communities. This volume, *Glimpses of Jewish Frankfurt*, is the second volume in this series. *Glimpses of Jewish Warsaw* was the inaugural volume. We have chosen Frankfurt as the second volume in the series to contrast the experiences of Eastern European Jewry, as represented by Warsaw, and Western European Jewry, as represented by Frankfurt. Future volumes offering glimpses of Vilna, Brisk, and Cracow have already been assigned and are in various stages of preparation. We also welcome submissions of manuscripts or proposals from authors who would like to undertake similar treatments of other prominent Jewish communities anywhere in the world.

We would like to take this opportunity to express our gratitude to the following talented people who have made the dream into a reality: Rabbi Yitzchak Alfasi, the popular and

15

learned Israeli author, who prepared the original Hebrew manuscript; Rabbi Avraham Yaakov Finkel, who translated the work with a high degree of professionalism; Rabbi Avraham Marmorstein, who edited the manuscript with his usual dexterity and skill; and Rabbi Aaron Perlow, who initiated, guided and coordinated the development of the work through its early stages. We would also like to acknowledge the "in-house" efforts of Art Director Deenee Cohen and Typographer Chaya Bleier, whose combined talents are reflected in the elegant production of this book.

In closing, we would like to express our humble gratitude to the *Ribono Shel Olam* for blessing our efforts in this important endeavor with success. We pray that our work bring honor to His Name and that our future efforts be blessed with equal success.

Y.Y.R.
Elul, 5753 (1993)
Lakewood, N.J.

JEWISH
Glimpses of
FRANKFURT

Chapter One

THE ANCIENT COMMUNITY

The proud tradition of the Jews of Frankfurt has its roots much earlier than most European communities. Frankfurt itself was one of the first centers of commerce and transportation to develop in Europe of antiquity. It was not that long before a nascent Jewish community formed, sowing the seeds of centuries of scholarship, generosity and piety.

Early History

The Jewish community of Frankfurt-am-Main, one of the oldest in Germany, has roots that go back to antiquity. The city is situated on the banks of the Main River and is called Frankfurt-am-Main to distinguish it from Frankfurt-an-der-Oder, a city on the older river fifty miles east of Berlin.

The history of the Jews of Frankfurt reflects much of the

fate of the entire Jewish people in exile. The chronicle of its community is marked by a cycle of putting down roots, later followed by persecution and expulsion. Yet amazingly, in spite of torment and oppression, the community regenerated itself again and again, burgeoning with an inexhaustible surge of creativity and a prodigious flowering of Jewish life. In Frankfurt, the prophetic paradox of *"bedamayich chayi*, in your blood, live!" (*Yechezkel* 16:6) became a palpable reality. It was there that the battle for the soul of the Jewish people was fought between Jews loyal to the Torah and assimilationists of various stripes and shades. It was there that a mighty resurgence of Torah-observant Judaism was sparked under the banner of "*Torah im Derech Eretz*," scrupulous adherence to Torah and *mitzvos* combined with secular knowledge.

For many years of its existence, Frankfurt was one of the foremost Jewish *kehillos* in Europe; indeed a number of the most illustrious sages served in its rabbinate.

With a tinge of envy, people in the eighteenth century would aptly describe Frankfurt as "a community that has no match; where even the night watchman is an accomplished Torah scholar." Justifiably proud, the Jews of Frankfurt would characterize their community as "the greatest in all of Germany, the goal of everyone's aspirations." Chauvinistically, they would ask, "*Es geht mir nicht in den Kopf hinein, wie kann ein Mensch nicht von Frankfurt sein?* I cannot get it through my head; how can anyone not come from Frankfurt?"

Present-day Frankfurt is the provincial capital of Hessen, with a permanent population of 670,000 inhabitants, augmented by 90,000 foreign workers. For centuries, the city has been a bustling center of commerce and banking. The Rothschilds, one of Frankfurt's prominent Jewish families, opened their first bank in Frankfurt in 1798. Today, it is the hub of banking and finance for all of Germany, as well as home to the Federal Bank of Germany.

Frankfurt holds two great trade fairs a year. The fair held in September opened first in 1240, and the February fair started in 1330. The September fair is cited in Jewish literature in the fifteenth century, when Rabbi Yosef Kolon, the Maharik, who served as *rav* at the time, addressed the issue of Jewish merchants participating in the fair on the days of *Chol Hamoed Sukkos*.

The downtown sector of Frankfurt, which was leveled in World War II by Allied bombers, has been rebuilt and boasts an opera-house, numerous museums and libraries. The foundation of its oldest building was laid in the ninth century, and remnants of towers and gates of the ancient city wall can still be seen today.

Frankfurt is a major center of transportation with three harbor areas and ranks third among Germany's inland ports. The city prides itself on having one of Europe's largest and busiest airports. It is easily accessible by automobile via the Autobahn super highway system from any part of Europe. A river and canal system link the city with the North Sea.

The origins of the earliest Jewish settlement of Frankfurt are shrouded in obscurity. Most historians believe that the city rose to eminence in the twelfth century, and that the first Jewish settlement dates back to that period. There are, however, a number of respected researchers who trace the origins of the initial Jewish settlement to a much earlier date.

There is no doubt that the city was first settled by Roman legionnaires. The shallow ford in the Main River provided the easiest north-south river crossing in all of Germany. After the fall of the Roman Empire, the Franks, a Germanic tribe living on the Rhine early in the Common Era, crossed the Main River to establish a settlement; hence, the city's name, which means "ford of the Franks." There is also historical proof that the French king Charlemagne spent the winter of 793 in Frankfurt.

According to the historians of the "early settlement"

school, Jews resided in Frankfurt as early as the sixth century. They lived scattered among the Christian population but later withdrew into their own neighborhood. Very little is known about these Jews. Merchants probably visited Frankfurt's annual fall fairs, subsequently took up residence there and formed the nucleus of a Jewish community. To bolster their contention of an early Jewish settlement, the proponents of this theory point to a document in which King Lothair I put a Jew on trial in Frankfurt in or before the year 885.

At any rate, there are indications that during the reign of Charlemagne (768-814) there was a Jewish presence in Frankfurt. A tradition is mentioned in *Teshuvos Maharshal 29* (Responsa of Rabbi Shlomo Luria, 1510-1573) that Charlemagne, who was favorably inclined toward the Jews, brought Rabbi Moshe Hazaken and his son Rabbi Klonymos to Mainz (twenty miles west of Frankfurt) from Lucca, Lombardy, in Northern Italy, to strengthen that ancient Jewish community.

More proof of a Jewish settlement in Frankfurt comes to us from the eleventh century, when in 1074, King Henry IV mentions Frankfurt among the towns where the Jews of Worms were permitted to trade without having to pay customs dues. Further evidence can be elicited from a contract dated one hundred years later by which a silversmith from Cologne bought one half of a house in Frankfurt belonging to a Jew named Gottschalk (a common German Jewish name meaning "servant of G-d").

The twelfth century provides the first evidence from Jewish sources attesting to the existence of a Jewish *kehillah* in Frankfurt. It is found in a *teshuvah* by Rabbi Eliezer ben Nassan (c. 1090-c. 1170), better known as the Raavan, a noted Tosafist and a contemporary of the Rashbam and Rabbeinu Tam. The Raavan served as the Rabbi of Mainz and was a leading figure in the conclave of one hundred and fifty rabbis held in Troyes in the year 1150, at which several important enactments were passed. In one of his responsa in his work *Even Haezer* (Prague, 1610), he rules as follows: "If people who live in one city visit another city and, while there, are ordered to make a contribution to the local *tzedakah* fund, they are required to comply and must donate the assessed amount. However, the money they contributed must be returned to them when they go home. [And since these funds were earmarked for charitable purposes] they must give the money to the poor people of their hometown. This ruling applies only to a city in which there is no rabbi, for example, the city of Frankfurt and others. [If the city has a rabbi, he is in charge of distributing the charity funds to the poor on behalf of the community.]"

For the purpose of our discussion we will not delve into the legal intricacies of this responsa. We can deduce from here that in the Raavan's time there evidently existed a *kehillah* in Frankfurt, although it had no rabbi as yet and was probably small.

Chapter Two

PERSECUTION AND EXPULSION

After Jewish communities in Western Europe became established in the tenth and eleventh centuries, gradually carving out a stable existence in relative harmony with their gentile neighbors, their survival was threatened by new dangers. Disguised as religious zeal, and fanned by greed, the flames of hatred swept across Western Europe in the twelfth and thirteenth centuries. Frankfurt was no exception.

The Crusades

There are other painful reminders of an early Jewish presence in Frankfurt—the records of bloody massacres and expulsions. The first large-scale outrage of this kind was perpetrated by the Crusaders, who killed thousands of Jews in the name of the "religion of love."

On November 26, 1095, in Clermont, France, Pope Urban II launched the First Crusade "to capture Jerusalem from the Moslems and subject it to Christendom." His declaration ignited a religious hysteria that swept through France and Germany. In the following year, 1096, a vast rabble of crude, superstitious peasants were marching toward the Rhine, heading for Jerusalem. As the mob made its way southward, they began attacking and pillaging the Jewish communities along the Rhine, killing eight hundred Jews in Worms, more than a thousand in Mainz, destroying the synagogue in Cologne and murdering the Jews of Speyer. The mob offered the Jews a choice of baptism or death. Most chose martyrdom. In all, about five thousand Jews died, and their communities were devastated.

The official chronicler of the carnage of the First Crusade has this to say about Frankfurt: "The Jewish community of Frankfurt, as well as Rabbi Ephraim bar Tamar and the students of his *yeshivah*,were all slain by the Crusaders."

The Massacre of 1241

Gradually, the Frankfurt community recovered, and during the twelfth century, it had an organized and flourishing *kehillah*, though still small in number. In the wake of the persecutions of the Jews in France by King Philip August II, many French Jews fled to Frankfurt after the year 1200. As a result of this influx, the community grew measurably, but by moving to Frankfurt the hapless refugees jumped out of the frying pan into the fire, as anti-Semitic harassment and indiscriminate arrests made life in Frankfurt intolerable. The excesses came to a bloody climax in the massacre and expulsion of 1241. The immediate cause of this bloodbath was the conversion of a Frankfurt Jew to Christianity. His apostasy created a storm of protest and dismay in the Jewish community. In retaliation for their expression of outrage, the Jews of Frankfurt were offered the choice of baptism or death. The entire community of nearly two hundred Jews refused baptism. Those who could not flee met with death at the hands of the murderous mob, and the Jewish quarter was destroyed. Among the victims were the rabbis, Rabbi Isaac Habachur Chazan and Rabbi Isaac ben Rabbi Nathan. The latter was martyred together with his wife Esther, his daughter Yuta, who was a bride, and his son Judah.

Around this time, there lived in Frankfurt a towering scholar, Rabbi Shimon Kara, known as Rabbi Shimon Hadarshan, author of the famous *Midrash*ic anthology *Yalkut Shimoni*. His work is a compilation of the ethical insights as they are expressed in the *Aggadic* literature. It is a work of inestimable value, because the author quotes numerous *aggados* and *midrashim* which have been lost or are not available to us. *Yalkut Shimoni* is our only source for these ancient *Aggadic* and *Midrash*ic writings. It has been said, "What the Rambam has done for *Halachah*, Rabbi Shimon has done for *Aggadah*."

A popular, old saying praised Rabbi Shimon Hadarshan in the following verses:

Rabbi Shimon an der Pfort
Kann die ganze Torah auf ein Wort.

Rabbi Shimon [who lives] at the [river] port,
Knows the whole Torah, word for word.

In the aftermath of the Frankfurt massacre of 1241, King Frederick II ordered an investigation which lasted several years. The end result was that the city administration was cleared of any wrongdoing, and the Jews were granted permission to return to Frankfurt. Their safety and protection was guaranteed by the treaty of 1256 between the Archbishop of Mainz and the Jews under his jurisdiction. This treaty provided that the Jews were "servants of the king" (*imperialis servi camerae*), imposing heavy penalties on anyone harming the Jews. The Church's benevolence was motivated by a two-fold reason. First, the coffers of the Church were filled by the exorbitant sums extorted from the Jews for this protection, and second, the Church was interested in preserving a remnant of Jews "as a living memorial to the suffering of the Nazarene."

By about 1270, Frankfurt had once again become an active Jewish community, centered in the Jewish quarter. The *kehillah* also established a Jewish cemetery at the outskirts of the city. This cemetery was in use until 1829, or close to six hundred years, and even survived the Nazi era. The oldest of its many ancient gravestones dates back to the year 1272. In 1952, two Jewish tombstones dated 1284 were discovered under the altar of the Frankfurt cathedral.

The *kehillah* was thriving once again, and the voice of Torah resounded anew in the narrow streets of the Jewish quarter as old and young immersed themselves in the study of Hashem's Word. Relations with the gentile population were peaceful, and under the relative safety of government protection, the future looked very bright.

Historical facts from this period are very scant, and only scattered data have been passed down to us. Tradition has it that, in 1292, King Adolf made an attempt to extort an enormous sum of money from the Jewish community, but his effort was thwarted by the Mayor of Frankfurt, Heinrich von Praunheim, who took the Jews under his wing and shielded them from their oppressive king.

The Maharam of Rothenburg

A tale of great self-sacrifice dating back to this period has as its hero a Jew from Frankfurt, Rabbi Shlomo Wimpfen.

27

The greatest Torah authority in Germany during the thirteenth century was Rabbi Meir of Rothenburg, better known as the Maharam of Rothenburg (c.1215-1293), whose rulings were considered binding throughout Germany. A prolific writer, his most famous work is the collection of his responsa, *Teshuvos Maharam* (Cremona, 1557).

To escape the harsh decrees of Emperor Rudolph I and the persecutions and massacres in Germany, thousands of Jews fled Germany. Among them was the Maharam, who decided to seek refuge in Italy.

On his way there, in Lombardy, he was recognized by the apostate Kneppe. Kneppe denounced him to the bishop of Basel who was passing through the town. Emperor Rudolph I had the Maharam imprisoned in the fortress at Ensisheim in Alsace hoping to obtain a huge ransom for his release. The money was raised, but the Maharam would not permit it to be paid in accordance with the ruling of the *Mishnah* (*Gittin* 4:6), so as not to set a precedent and encourage the rulers to imprison other leaders.

After spending seven years in prison, where he continued his learning and teaching from memory, the Maharam died there in 1293. The government refused to release his body for an additional fourteen years.

At last, through the efforts of Rabbi Shlomo Wimpfen of Frankfurt, who magnanimously spent most of his fortune to gain the release of the body, the Maharam of Rothenburg was laid to rest in the Worms cemetery. In return, Rabbi Shlomo Wimpfen asked only to be buried next to the illustrious *gaon*.

Upon Rabbi Shlomo's death, on the fourth of *Adar,* 1307, his request was fulfilled. The two tombstones standing side by side offer mute testimony to the union of Torah and *gemilus chasadim*, the pillars that sustain the Jewish people during the long exile.

A great luminary from this era who served as Rabbi of Frankfurt was Rabbi Alexander Zuslein Hakohen (died in

1348), author of *Sefer Agudah* (Cracow, 1571), a famous compendium of rabbinical decisions of the most prominent commentators. The work covers most of Talmudic law and also contains a large number of the author's own expositions and practical *halachic* decisions.

Although the second period of growth of the Frankfurt *kehillah* was relatively short, it produced a remarkable flowering of Torah and its sages.

The Black Death

This era of great promise was brought to an abrupt end by a small furry creature: the rat. Rats originating in Mongolia had been infected by the deadly bacillus *Pasteurella pestis*. Moving westward along the caravan routes, disease-carrying rodents arrived on a trading ship in Genoa, Italy, in December of 1347.

Two days after the ship docked, an epidemic of bubonic plague broke out. It spread swiftly across Italy, France, Germany, Russia and England, killing almost half the population of Europe, about seventy-five million, in three years. Historians have named the deadly disease the Black Death. No one understood what was causing the malady, and gripped by panic, people hysterically sought a cause for the horror. Jews, who observe rigid standards of personal cleanliness and hygiene (washing many times each day and regularly immersing in a *mikveh*), died in much smaller numbers than the general population. It did not take long before people began to accuse Jews of plotting to poison the world.

In 1349, Jews in Lausanne, Switzerland, were tortured and made to confess to poisoning the drinking water, and the rumor spread throughout Europe. The clergy whipped up the masses with fiery tirades.

The wildly aroused mob pillaged, burned and massacred,

engulfing two hundred communities in Germany with blood-thirsty hatred. Six thousand Jews died in Mainz. The Jews of Berne, Switzerland, were burned to death. Six hundred Jews in Basel and two thousand Jews in Strassburg were buried alive; ironically, the men were granted permission to wear their *talleisim* as they went to their deaths. The Jewish communities of Colmar (Alsace), Zurich, Speyer, Muehlhausen and Erfurt were butchered.

The Jews of Frankfurt were massacred on *Erev Tishah b'Av*, 1349, and the community was completely wiped out. Some historians believe that Rabbi Alexander Zuslein, the Rabbi of Frankfurt, perished in the massacre of his hometown Erfurt.

When the plague abated in 1351, Europe had been devastated. Tens of thousands of Jews had been brutally murdered, and their *kehillos* lay in ruin.

The burnings and killings in the wake of the Black Death followed a well-established pattern, for only fourteen years earlier, in 1337, bands of peasants had roamed for three years through Alsace, the Rhienland, Bavaria and Austria, killing Jews and wreaking havoc on one hundred and fourteen Jewish communities.

Since these cutthroats wore leather armbands, they were called Armleder gangs. Their reign of terror ended when the administrators of the various cities, fearing for their own safety, drove off the hoodlums and so, many *kehillos* were saved.

Unfortunately, this miracle was not repeated during the Black Death massacres, which were allowed to run their bloody course unhampered by any sort of government intervention.

For Frankfurt, the massacre of 1349 marked the second time the community was destroyed. Before that catastrophe, the Frankfurt community had gained a place of prominence among the chain of ancient German *kehillos* on the banks of the Rhine River that reached from Cologne south to Mainz, Worms and Speyer. Now all its achievements had been ravaged with fire and sword.

Regeneration and Consolidation

With astounding vitality, only eleven years after the Black Death massacres of 1349, the Frankfurt *kehillah* rose from its ashes. In 1360, Frankfurt reopened its gates to Jews. In 1363, three years after the reestablishment of the Frankfurt community, the *kehillah* was again served by a spiritual leader. All we know about him is that his name was Rabbi Joseph Lampe. Likewise, very little is known about his successor, Rabbi Asher.

During this period, the Jewish community lived in constant fear, the threat of violent death hanging over their heads at all times. It is interesting to note, as a sign of the times, that Rabbi Asher composed in 1374 a very moving prayer to be said before dying a martyr's death *al kiddush Hashem*, for the sanctification of Hashem's Name. The prayer ends with the words, "Blessed are You Hashem, our Lord, King of the Universe, Who has sanctified us with His commandments and has commanded us to love with all our heart and all our soul His glorious and awesome Name, Who was, Who is and Who will be forever."

Rabbi Asher's final instruction to those who are about to die is, "As one submits to death one exclaims, '*Shema Yisrael*, Hear, O Yisrael, Hashem is our Lord, Hashem is One.'"

In 1385, Rabbi Meir Nordhausen, son of the martyred Shmuel, is mentioned as Rabbi of the Frankfurt community.

In 1394, the *kehillah* was led by Rabbi Susslin of Speyer. Mentioned also as officiating rabbi is Rabbi Meir of Fulda. Among the headstones in the cemetery there is one of Rabbi Yaakov Katz who died in 1397.

During this period, a highly acclaimed rabbi was Rabbi Nathan Halevi Epstein, who officiated in Frankfurt from 1430 until 1460. Speaking on behalf of his community, Rabbi Epstein raised serious objections to a number of statutes that had been adapted at a rabbinical conference in Bingen. When his friends Rabbi Moshe Mintz and Rabbi Febes of Cologne joined him in opposing the measures, the sponsors withdrew the statutes "in view of the opposition of such eminent personages."

Other famous Frankfurt rabbinical personalities from this period were Rabbi Meshullam Zalman Epstein (known as Semel Epstein), who was a famous *shtadlan* that pleaded the cause of the Jewish people before the authorities, and his friend Rabbi Bing Oppenheim. Rabbi Epstein, who had a deep attachment to Torah, supported six young scholars who studied at his house.

As an interesting sidelight, it should be pointed out that the family name Epstein has its roots in Spain. The original name of the family was Benveniste. In the wake of the expulsions from Spain, the family fled to Germany where they settled in the town of Epstein and adopted that name.

Chapter Three

DEFENSIVE BARRICADES

The first generations of Jews to settle in the cities and towns of Western Europe made their homes wherever they could find the opportunity to buy land. Although subject to frequent and troublesome exiles and restrictions, they were nonetheless rarely confined to a particular, sequestered part of the town.

After the first ghettoes were devised in the Catholic states of the northern parts of Italy, eager church authorities copied the idea all over the continent, driven by insatiable avarice and a profound and abiding antipathy towards the Jewish people. Professing fear of the powerful influence of the Jewish faith, the church fathers often enriched themselves with exorbitant fees for every departure and every market stall outside the ghetto walls.

However, the secluded homes behind the defensive barricade of the ghetto walls became great concentrations of

Torah and communal life, thus benefiting from the cruelly imposed isolation.

Crowded Quarters

In 1442, the emperor and the church authorities, including the Pope himself, demanded that the Jews of Frankfurt be restricted to living in a separate area. For twenty years the city administration fought the creation of a ghetto, but ultimately the emperor and the Church prevailed. In 1462, the Jews of Frankfurt were transferred to a specially constructed street called Judengasse, which remained their home for three hundred years. Since the ghetto was never permitted to expand beyond its original area, the existing houses were subdivided and extended, and additional stories were built, creating bizarre-looking streets with tall houses hovering over narrow winding lanes, shutting out the daylight.

Although the Jews in the ghetto were subjected to severe physical and social hardship, the community developed even more intensely. There were one hundred and two inhabitants of the ghetto in 1431, two hundred and fifty in 1520, nine hundred in 1569, twelve hundred in 1580, twenty-two hundred in 1600 and about three thousand in 1610.

The community could point with pride at the institutions it maintained, including a synagogue, called Altschul, a *beis midrash*, a *mikveh*, a wedding hall, hospitals and a cemetery. The administration of the *kehillah* was under the direction of the rabbi and the board of elders who assisted him.

The eminent stature of the rabbis who served Frankfurt during the fifteenth and sixteenth centuries marks Frankfurt as one of the foremost Jewish communities. Notable among these are the following personalities.

Rabbi Nathan Halevi Epstein was succeeded (about 1460) by Rabbi Shimon Hakohen, who is mentioned in the writings of the famous Rabbi Yosef Colon (1410-1480) of Italy, better known as the Maharik. In a *teshuvah* (number twenty-one), the Maharik expresses his high regard for Rabbi Shimon. A headstone in the old Frankfurt cemetery bears the inscription, "the great sage, Rabbi Shimon Hakohen." The ravages of time and weather have erased the rest of the inscription. The only legible words remaining are, "... Lament, head of Yisrael, Ark of the Torah."

Rabbi Shimon was succeeded by Rabbi Yisrael Rheinbach "who disseminated Torah in Yisrael" and who died in 1505.

After Rabbi Rheinbach's death, the rabbinate passed to Rabbi Yitzchak ben Elyakim, who served the community for more than thirty-five years. In 1510, during his tenure, a great number of rabbinic *sefarim* were confiscated in Frankfurt at the instigation of the infamous apostate Pfefferkorn. He maligned the Talmud before the Dominican monks, claiming that it was full of derogatory statements against Christianity. In 1509, Emperor Maximilian, on the advice of his sister who had become a nun, issued an edict by which all Jewish books were to be confiscated.

The Jews of Frankfurt enlisted the help of Rabbi Yosef Yoselman of Rosheim, a descendant of Rashi and a well-known *shtadlan,* to intercede on their behalf. The correspondence concerning this matter is still in existence. In the end, the emperor appointed a committee of scholars headed by Johannes Reuchlin to examine the contents of the books of the Talmud.

Reuchlin (1455-1522), a Christian humanist and noted scholar of the Hebrew language, was an admirer of the Talmud and rabbinic literature. He sent a highly favorable expert opinion to the Archbishop of Mainz, in whose diocese Frankfurt was located and who was in charge of the disposition of the books of the Frankfurt community. Reuchlin's opinion did not sit well with the Dominican priests, who now launched a long and acrimonious campaign against Reuchlin, denying his competence. In rebuttal, Reuchlin published a work entitled *Augenspiegel* (1511), in which he demonstrated the contemptible ignorance of Pfefferkorn and the illiteracy of the Dominican monks who supported him. This book was to have a major influence in advancing the movement of the German Protestant Reformation.

Rabbi Yoselman of Rosheim

The following fascinating story relates the details of the discussion Rabbi Yosef Yoselman of Rosheim had with the Archbishop of Mainz, in which he convinced the archbishop of the evil character and ignorance of Pfefferkorn. It is told in *Sarei Hameiah* and is attributed to Rabbi Avraham Yitzchak Kook. It is also cited in *Rabbi Yosef Yoselman of Rosheim*, by Rabbi Marcus Lehmann (London, 1974).

An unemployed butcher from Moravia by the name of Pfefferkorn (1469-1524) had been arrested in Frankfurt in an attempted burglary. As a result of his thievery, he was expelled from the Jewish community. To exact revenge, Pfefferkorn abandoned the Jewish faith and converted to Catholicism, adopting the name Johann. Johann boasted to the Dominican monks who baptized him that he had been a rabbi and was well-versed in Talmudic literature. At the urging of the Dominicans, Emperor Maximilian granted Pfefferkorn the authority to confiscate and burn the books of the Talmud and rabbinic *sefarim*.

When Rabbi Yosef Yoselman of Rosheim (a town in eastern France), the great *shtadlan*, learned of the impending disaster, he approached the Archbishop of Mainz, imploring him to persuade the emperor to rescind the decree. In the course of their conversation, Rabbi Yosef described to the archbishop the corrupt character of Pfefferkorn.

"Look, your excellency," Rabbi Yosef said. "All the trash

we discard, you Christians are eager to pick up."

In the ensuing discussion, Rabbi Yosef tried to convince the archbishop to invite Pfefferkorn to test his knowledge of the Talmud.

"You will see that I'm right," he concluded.

"But, Rabbi," the archbishop replied with a smile, "I don't know the first thing about your Talmud. How do you expect me to test him?"

"It won't take me more than half an hour to teach you one chapter in the Talmud by which to test Pfefferkorn and determine how well-acquainted he is with the subject matter."

"All right, Rabbi," the archbishop replied. "Go ahead, teach me. I'm willing to try."

"In our Talmud," Rabbi Yosef began, "in the tractate *Gittin* (51a), the rabbis explore the question of *hezeik she'eino nikkar*, meaning, whether or not you must pay compensation if you caused 'invisible damage' to someone's property."

Rabbi Yosef wrote on a piece of paper in German script the words *hezeik she'eino nikkar*.

"But tell me, Rabbi," the archbishop asked, "if the damage is invisible and unnoticeable, then there is no damage at all!"

"Your excellency is right. At first glance it seems that there is no basis for the entire inquiry. But let me explain the underlying meaning of these words. Consider for example the following case. When the holy Temple was standing in Jerusalem we needed a *parah adumah*, a red heifer. Let me write down these words also in German script. According to the Bible, the ashes of this red heifer were needed to purify a ritually unclean person. But this red heifer could be used only if it was completely red, had no defect, never had carried a yoke and had never performed any labor. Of course, a heifer that met all these requirements was extremely rare and very expensive, and a person in whose herd a red heifer was born could demand a price of thousands of gold pieces.

"Imagine, your excellency, if someone were fortunate enough to own a red heifer like this, he could expect to become rich overnight. Now let us assume that his neighbor furtively placed a yoke on the animal and made it pull a plow for a few minutes. Certainly, the slight amount of work the animal performed caused no visible damage to it. The cow looked just as perfect after pulling the plow as it did before. Nevertheless, according to the Bible, it cannot be used as a *parah adumah* any longer. The cow which had a value of thousands of gold pieces is now worth only a few hundred pieces of silver, no more than any ordinary cow in the market. This is what the Talmud means by *hezeik she'eino nikkar*, 'invisible damage.'

"Now the juridical question arises as to whether the person causing the damage must pay for the decrease in value of the cow, or whether he could argue, 'Look here, I'm returning your cow in its original condition, without any flaw or blemish. Why should I have to pay damages?'"

The archbishop of Mainz listened attentively.

"This is an interesting legal question," he said. "I'm curious to know, how was this case decided?"

"The Rambam, one of our greatest legal minds," Rabbi Yosef replied, "has ruled in his Code (*Hilchos Choveil Umazik*, chapter 7), 'If a person causes invisible damage to his neighbor's property, since the article has not changed, nor has its appearance been marred, according to Biblical law he is exempt from paying compensation.' Let me also write down in German script the name of the legal authority, Maimonides.

"I think," the rabbi continued, "that this Talmudic legal case will be sufficient to examine Pfefferkorn and to verify how little he knows of the Talmud."

The archbishop reviewed the Hebrew expressions that had been spelled out on the sheet of paper several times. After making sure that the archbishop pronounced them correctly, Rabbi Yosef left, his heart filled with hope and faith.

Pfefferkorn was summoned to appear in person before the Archbishop of Mainz. Strutting into the archbishop's study, he bragged about having confiscated hundreds of volumes of the Talmud from the Jews of Frankfurt.

"Tell me, Pfefferkorn," asked the archbishop. "Is it true that you studied all the books of the Talmud as you claim you did? And did you really find in them nothing but scorn and abuse against the Christian religion?"

"Why certainly, your excellency," the *meshumad* replied arrogantly. "I used to be a rabbi, and I remember by heart almost every page of the Talmud. I give you my word—the word of a faithful Christian—that the entire Talmud from beginning to end is full of disdain and ridicule of Christianity. That's what the Talmud is all about!"

"It seems to me that you are exaggerating," the archbishop said with barely suppressed indignation. "As I know, the Talmud contains also discourses on the subject of litigation and adjudication of monetary disputes."

"Quite true," Pfefferkorn interrupted brazenly. "We do, indeed, find many legalistic discussions on money matters; on how to cheat Christians, how to swindle and defraud them and rob them of their last penny."

"But I know of legal cases in the Talmud that have no bearing at all on Christianity," the archbishop shot back, his eyes flashing angrily. "For example, I know of the Talmudic deliberations on the topic of *hezeik she'eino nikkar*. Do you, Pfefferkorn, remember this case, and how it was decided?"

Visibly shaken and confused, the *meshumad* began to stammer, "*Hezeik she'eino nikkar . . . hezeik she'eino nikkar . . .*"

He tried to recall the Talmud lessons from his long-forgotten *cheder* years. Suddenly, a phrase with a familiar ring popped into his head. *Hezeik she'eino nikkar lav shemei hezeik.* Invisible damage is not considered damage.

"There you have it, your excellency," he called out quite

triumphantly. "Here is your proof of what the Talmud teaches. 'Go ahead, do harm to others, cheat them, mislead them, steal from them; just make sure they don't notice it . . . Place your good merchandise on top of the pile, and put the damaged goods on the bottom. As long as the buyer is not aware that you are cheating him, you are exempt from making restitution.'"

The archbishop could no longer contain his anger.

"Why, you miserable, despicable liar! You mudslinging swindler!" he exclaimed, seething with fury. "That's how you deceived the emperor with your empty claims of knowing the Talmud and duped him into authorizing you to burn the Talmud. Now I recognize your total ignorance and your boundless gall. You are nothing but a contemptible fraud. *Hezeik she'eino nikkar* has nothing to do with stealing or misleading. It means that the external appearance of the damaged article has not changed, like in the case of a *parah adumah* which has been put to work, but which remains outwardly perfect and unchanged. It is only due to Biblical law that the cow became invalid and its value diminished. The meaning of *hezeik she'eino nikkar* is that according to Jewish law, as set forth by the codifier Maimonides, the person who caused such 'invisible damage' is exempt from making restitution. But you, Pfefferkon, you are a 'rebellious son' of your people. I demand that you return forthwith the books of the Talmud you confiscated under false pretenses, for you tricked the emperor and his cabinet. Get out of here! And stop annoying us with your lies and your dirty tricks."

Sixteenth and Seventeenth Century Rabbis

A number of highly respected rabbis officiated in Frankfurt during the sixteenth century. Among these are:

Rabbi Naftali Hertz Treves (died c. 1556), a prominent

kabbalist, who gained renown as the author of the *Kabbalah Siddur*, first published in 1560. In his commentary to the *siddur*, he expounded on the Kabbalistic meaning of the *tefillos*. (Incidentally, the well-known German Jewish families called Dreyfuss originated in Treves, from which their name is derived.)

Rabbi Yehudah ben Yitzchak Halevi of Frankfurt wrote an introduction to the seminal work *Sefer Halachos Gedolos* (Venice, 1548).

Rabbi Eliezer Treves (died after 1560), the son of Rabbi Naftali Hertz Treves was acclaimed as a great *halachic* authority throughout Europe. His universal repute is evident in an answer given by Rabbi Yochanan Treves of Venice. Rabbi Yochanan was asked to render a *halachic* decision regarding a dispute over a *get* that had been written in Prague, and he proposed that the matter be adjudicated by three eminent German rabbis he would name. The first name he suggested was that of Rabbi Eliezer Treves of Frankfurt.

On a visit to Cracow, Rabbi Eliezer Treves formed a close acquaintance with the rabbi of that city, Rabbi Moshe Isserles, the illustrious Rema (c.1520-c.1572). The Rema, famous for his glosses to the *Shulchan Aruch*, said about Rabbi Eliezer, "His eminence is such that his opinion should be followed on all Torah questions." The Rema expressed his high regard for Rabbi Eliezer and the scholars of Frankfurt, stating, "In my eyes, the rabbis of Frankfurt are comparable to the Sages of Yavneh." (*Teshuvos Rema*, Responsum 91)

Among Rabbi Eliezer's students was the historian Rabbi David Gans, author of *Tzemach David*, a historical chronology (Prague, 1592). He also studied under the Rema, and he died in Prague in 1613.

An outstanding student of Rabbi Eliezer Treves was Rabbi Akiva Frankfurter, a spellbinding preacher whose sermons always drew very large audiences. He was a gifted composer of *tefillos* and *piyutim*. Many of his creations have been

41

published by his disciple Rabbi Eliyahu Loanz under the title *Zemiros Vesishbachos* (Basel, 1599). His father-in-law was the fabulously wealthy and pious Shimon Gunzburg. When Rabbi Akiva died in 1597, the celebrated Maharal of Prague bemoaned his passing in a moving eulogy which appeared in print (Prague, 1598).

Rabbi Avraham Naftali Hertz succeeded Rabbi Eliezer Treves. He wrote a commentary on the *Sefer Maharil,* which was incorporated into later editions. He died in 1599.

Rabbi Shmuel ben Eliezer of Friedberg succeeded his father-in-law Rabbi Avraham Naftali Hertz as *rav* of Frankfurt. He hosted an important rabbinic conference in Frankfurt in 1603, at which a number of important decrees were enacted. Among these were: all *shochtim* must be tested; the prohibition against non-kosher wine was strengthened; a warning was issued against drinking in non-Jewish taverns; and it was established that a rabbi should render decisions only in his own district. Another decision reached at the conference has been widely adhered to until our own time—that no book should be printed without the *haskamos* of three rabbis of towns. Rabbi Shmuel died on *Tzom Gedaliah,* 1609.

By this time, the *kehillah* had risen to such prominence that it could attract prodigious Torah scholars. The next *rav* of Frankfurt was Rabbi Yeshayah Halevi Horowitz (c.1560-1630), the author of the highly acclaimed *Shenei Luchos Habris* (Amsterdam, 1648), popularly known as the Shelah Hakadosh (Shelah being the acronym of the initials of the title of his book). The book is a compendium of the six hundred and thirteen laws of the Torah. The author interprets the *mitzvos* from a Kabbalistic point of view and analyzes the ethical aspects of each *mitzvah.*

The Shelah held rabbinical posts in important Torah centers such as Ostroh, Posen and Cracow, before coming to Frankfurt. He stayed in Frankfurt for eight years, from 1606 until 1614, the year in which the Jewish community fled the city in the wake of the Fettmilch rebellion. He returned to his hometown Prague, where he was elected rabbi. In 1622, he moved to Jerusalem and died in Veria in 1630.

Chapter Four

DIFFICULT TIMES

In the early seventeenth century, Frankfurt's Jews again faced the threat of destruction. Their survival of this threat was truly miraculous, and it reassured them that their prayers had been well answered. They commemorated their own miracle by proclaiming it a local *"Purim."*

The Frankfurt Purim

The seventeenth century had ominous beginnings for the Jews of Frankfurt. Immediately after the coronation of Emperor Mattias in 1612, a group of disgruntled guild craftsmen and small traders, who were in debt to Jews, petitioned the City Council to expel the Jews, who, in their words, "are living off the blood of the citizens [by charging interest on their loans]." The Council replied that the Jewish people were scrupulous in observing the laws against usury, and rather than placing the blame for their misery on the Jews, they should manage their finances more carefully and not incur heavy debts. However, the more the Council supported the Jews, the angrier grew the mood of the citizenry. The *kehillah*, fearful of what lay in store for them, turned to Hashem in prayer, repentance and fasting.

The unrest erupted into open rebellion when in 1614, Vincent Fettmilch organized a mob and attacked the ghetto, robbing and pillaging the Jewish houses. All the Jews fled the city, but the emperor outlawed the rebels, and their leaders were arrested and executed in 1616. Subsequently, the Jews were brought back to the ghetto with pomp and ceremony, an event annually commemorated by the Frankfurt *kehillah* on the twentieth of *Adar*.

Rabbi Yosef Hahn, *dayan* of Frankfurt and author of *Yosef Ometz*, describes the events in the following words:

"We declared a fast for the twenty-seventh of *Elul*, since on this day we were expelled from our community by the rebels. They deliberated whether to kill us or to drive us out, and they decided to spare our lives but to expel us from the city. The rebels robbed us of all our possessions and destroyed anything that remained. In our street they put to the torch countless holy books they had found in our homes and in the shul; they did not even respect the sanctity of our *Sifrei Torah*—because of our sins. . .

"The unfortunate refugees found shelter in the neighboring towns, where they received a friendly welcome. Finding strength in their faith in Hashem's compassion and in the knowledge of their innocence, they looked forward to better times. Before long, they were permitted to enter their hometown on a temporary basis, particularly at the time of the fair in August 1615 . . .

"And on February 28, 1616, the civil rights of the returnees were reinstated in a solemn ceremony."

Rabbi Hahn continues his report.

"We declared the twentieth of *Adar* as a day of feasting, to be called *Purim Vincenz* (named after Vincent Fettmilch) in *Yisrael*, consistent with the establishment of the *Purim* festival after the days of battles and wonders [in the days of Mordechai and Esther]. Indeed, miracles did happen to us on this day, for the commissioners of the Dukes of Mainz and Darmstadt—may Hashem exalt their glory—escorted us into our streets with full honors, accompanied by a large battalion of soldiers in battle dress, bearing flags and banners. They were led by a marching band with drums and trombones . . .

"The entire population, seeing the honor accorded us by the commissioners, stared with open-mouthed amazement; no one made a derogatory remark against us. On the contrary, they helped us remove the rubble that had accumulated near the gate of our street. This was necessary in order to clear a path for the two chariots, one of which bore the imperial standard—the one with the large eagle, the other carried my father-in-law Reb Avraham Breitingen, the *gabbai* of the Jewish community, who suffered from gout and was unable to walk. May Hashem grant us that we live to see the fulfillment of the prophecy (*Chaggai* 2:9), 'The glory of this latter House shall be greater than that of the former one.'"

Rabbi Hahn's prayer was answered, and as *dayan,* he played a major role in restoring the *kehillah* and guiding it into an era of unprecedented spiritual growth. This is all the more surprising in view of the restrictions that were imposed on the Jews, allowing a maximum of five hundred families to live in the ghetto and only twelve marriage licenses annually.

Rabbi Yosef Yuspa Norlingen Hahn (his full name) was born in Frankfurt around the year 1570 and served as head *dayan* of the *kehillah*. A man of unshakable faith in Hashem, he was greatly revered by his community for his erudition and sound judgment. He is famous for the book he wrote, titled *Yosef Ometz*, dealing with all the laws governing Jewish life, with particular emphasis on the distinct *minhagim* of Frankfurt.

The name Hahn is derived from the emblem that marked the family house, called Zum rothen Hahn, displaying a red rooster.

Rabbi Yosef Hahn died in Frankfurt in 1637.

After the restoration of the community in 1616, the *kehillah* did not immediately choose a *rav*, and only in 1618 was the post filled by Rabbi Shmuel Hildesheim, who united the community and led it on its path to recovery. With his organizational skill, Rabbi Hildesheim shaped the *kehillah*, giving it its distinct character, and launching it on the road to greatness. His varied activities fully occupied his time so that he left no writings. He died in 1628.

Rabbi Hildesheim was succeeded by Rabbi Pesachyah, who made no major changes in the structure of the *kehillah*. He was instrumental in publishing *Sefer Hakavanos* by Rabbi Chaim Vital, the great kabbalist. In Rabbi Pesachyah's words, "It is a book containing *sodos niflaos*, wondrous mysteries." The publication of this work, which is an introduction to the Kabbalistic teachings of the Ari Hakadosh, was endorsed by Rabbi Hahn and other prominent rabbis. Rabbi Pesachyah wrote an appendix to *Sefer Hakavanos* listing textual corrections. Rabbi Hahn reports in his *Yosef Ometz* that the *Sefer Hakavanos* had illegally been taken out of Eretz Yisrael. Because of the great sanctity of the book, its exportation had been banned by the rabbis of Eretz Yisrael, in an attempt to prevent the study of Kabbalah outside the Holy Land. According to its title page, the book was published in Venice in 1620. In fact, it was published in Hanau in 1624.

Subsequent to his tenure in Frankfurt, Rabbi Pesachyah officiated in the rabbinate of Worms and Nikolsburg. He died in 1637.

The next Chief Rabbi of Frankfurt was Rabbi Chaim Kohen of Prague, a scion of a celebrated family of scholars, who was appointed chief rabbi in 1628. He was a grandson of Rabbi Yehudah Loew, the illustrious Maharal of Prague (1526-1609). His sister Chavah was a scholarly woman who wrote commentaries on the *Siddur*, *Midrash* and *Targum*. He moved to Posen, and in 1632, Rabbi Shabsai Horowitz (1590-1660), son of the Shelah, was appointed to the rabbinate.

In his work *Vavei Haamudim*, an extensive introduction to his father's *Shenei Luchos Habris* (Shelah), Rabbi Shabsai characterized Frankfurt as "the greatest *kehillah* in Germany, whose scholars probe the depths of *halachah* like Tosafists." *Vavei Haamudim* is a collection of sermons focusing on the six "pillars of the world"—peace, justice, truth, Torah study, service of Hashem and kind deeds.

In the chapter on *avodah*, Rabbi Shabsai Horowitz vehemently admonished those "who recite their prayers without understanding or feeling, simply mouthing the words routinely."

He continues, "When I served as Rabbi of Frankfurt, I instituted a beneficial program whereby people are taught the *tefillos* of the entire year in a number of study groups, so that they should not just twitter like birds when they *daven*. For only a prayer that is said with understanding and concentration rises up to Heaven."

He had good things to say about some of the practices of his former community. "I praise the German Jews who set aside one tenth of their income for the poor. They are extremely stringent in the observance of this *mitzvah*, and this merit has caused them to be able to inherit and pass along great wealth from generation to generation."

In 1642, he was chosen as Rabbi of Posen, where he founded a *yeshivah*. In 1654, he moved to Vienna, where he remained until his death in 1660.

A prominent figure in Frankfurt around this time was Dr. Yosef Shlomo Delmedigo of Kandia (Crete), who served as the physician of the Jewish community. A highly skilled doctor, he distinguished himself for his wide knowledge of Torah, as well as physics and mathematics. He studied medicine and science at the University of Padua, where his mentor was the great Florentine astronomer Galileo Galilei (1564-1642). Delmedigo practiced medicine in a number of countries including Egypt, Turkey and Romania, and he served as the private physician of Count Radziwil of Poland. In 1648, he moved to Prague, where he died in 1655. The inscription on his tombstone reads,

"In all the world, he is the best,
There is no one like him, north, south, east or west."

Rabbi Menachem Bachrach was the president of the Frankfurt *kehillah* (1574-1580).

Rabbi Shimon Unsburg, the author of *Devek Tov*, a compilation of commentaries on difficult passages in Rashi (Venice, 1588), served as rabbi in Frankfurt.

Maharam Schiff and His Successors

Until this time, all the chief rabbis of Frankfurt had been imported from other great centers of Torah learning. The first native son to officiate in this post was Rabbi Meir Schiff (1608-1644). A brilliant scholar with an incisive and analytical mind, he was a bright meteor, swiftly flashing across the expanse of Torah scholarship. In his brief life of only thirty-six years, he achieved immortality.

At the tender age of seventeen, this deeply G-d-fearing prodigy was appointed Rabbi of Fulda. It was there that he wrote his universally acclaimed *chiddushim* on the *Gemara*, known as Maharam Schiff. The fact that they are printed in most major editions of the Talmud attests to the author's phenomenal greatness.

In 1644, Rabbi Meir Schiff was elected Chief Rabbi of the

prestigious *kehillah* of Prague. Tragically, he died soon after arriving in that city at thirty-six years of age, "like the sun setting before its time" (according to the words written on his gravestone).

After the departure of the Maharam Schiff, his father Rabbi Yaakov Schiff was chosen as *rosh yeshivah* of Frankfurt, and only after his death in 1644, was Rabbi Mendel Bass appointed as the new chief rabbi. Rabbi Mendel Bass, the foremost *talmid* of Rabbi Yoel Sirkis (the Bach, 1561-1640), was a recognized *halachic* authority and possessed a wide knowledge in the mysteries of Kabbalah.

Kabbalah had always been considered a field of study reserved for a few saintly scholars who followed an ascetic and other-worldly lifestyle. It was not meant for the masses. Yet, in 1653, Rabbi Naftali of Frankfurt published a book, *Emek Hamelech* (Amsterdam, 1653), in which he revealed the "mysteries" of Kabbalah, making them accessible to a wide circle of readers. When Rabbi Mendel Bass wrote a *haskamah* endorsing the book, this created a furor of controversy in the Frankfurt community. However, Rabbi Mendel was held in such extremely high esteem that the storm soon died down.

Under his leadership, the *yeshivah* of Frankfurt produced several world-renowned scholars. Among these were Rabbi Yair Chaim Bachrach of Worms, author of *Chavas Yair,* and Rabbi Meir Stern, a prominent Kabbalist who was Rabbi Mendel's son-in-law and later became Rabbi of Amsterdam. Rabbi Mendel Bass died on *Erev Sukkos*, 1666.

Rabbi Aharon Shmuel Kaidanover

It was a time of terror and trepidation for the Jews of Eastern Europe as a whirlwind of fire and fury swept across the Polish steppes.

In 1648, a Cossack chieftain named Bogdan Chmielnicki led a rabble of Ukrainian peasants in a mass uprising against their Polish overlords. Joined by Tartar hordes, they vented their pent-up wrath on the defenseless Jews. With savage fury they ravaged the countryside, burning, torturing and killing indiscriminately. The bloodthirsty mob maimed and massacred men, women and children and mutilated their remains. Between 1648 and 1653, more than one hundred thousand Jews died at the hands of the Cossacks, and three hundred communities were destroyed.

A detailed history of the entire tragic epoch was written by Rabbi Nassan Nota Hanover and is entitled *Yeven Metzulah* (Venice, 1743).

The Chmielnicki slaughter was the greatest massacre since the destruction of the *Beis Hamikdash* until the mass murders of Hitler's holocaust. The years 1648 and 1649 are remembered in everlasting infamy as *Gezeras Tach Vetat* (5448/5449).

At that time, there lived a great Torah scholar in Vilna, Rabbi Aharon Shmuel Kaidanover (1614-1676), who served as *dayan* in the *Beis Din* of Vilna together with the Shach. When the Cossacks invaded Vilna, he fled to Lublin, "wading through the stream of blood of my martyred brothers," as he describes his escape. But the Cossacks did not spare Lublin either. In the ensuing massacre, his two daughters were killed, his son narrowly escaped death, and Rabbi Aharon Shmuel himself was wounded. After experiencing many miracles, he arrived in Nikolsburg and moved to Fuerth where he served as rabbi. Subsequently, he was elected Chief Rabbi of Frankfurt.

His manuscripts were destroyed in Vilna, but he later wrote *Birkas Hazevach* (Amsterdam 1669), a treatise on *Kadashim*, and *Emunas Shmuel*, a collection of responsa (Frankfurt, 1663).

In 1671, when the prestigious *kehillah* of Cracow chose

him as their rabbi, he left Frankfurt after eleven years. He remained in Cracow until the end of his life.

Rabbi Yeshayah Halevi Horowitz II

In 1678, the Frankfurt community elected Rabbi Yeshayah Halevi Horowitz II, the grandson of the Shelah, as the new chief rabbi. In the latter half of the seventeenth century, Frankfurt had become a community of scholars and sages who immersed themselves exclusively in the study of Talmud and *halachah*. The research in Kabbalah was only pursued by a small minority and in private. No doubt, this was due to the disastrous episode of the false *mashiach* Shabsai Tzvi who died in 1676 after converting to Islam.

Shabsai Tzvi, whose emergence raised the hopes of the Jewish masses to a feverish pitch, based his teachings on fraudulent interpretations of Kabbalistic writings. After marching in triumph through the cities of Europe and the Near East and receiving the adulation of the Jewish masses, the imposter was unmasked. The disillusionment that followed his exposure as a false *mashiach* was a tragedy of cataclysmic proportions.

As a result of Shabsai Tzvi's misuse of Kabbalah, the study of *nistar* was strongly discouraged, and publication of Kabbalistic books was restricted.

Around this time, Rabbi David Grunhut of Wiesbaden and Frankfurt prepared for the publication of *Sefer Hagilgulim*, an important Kabbalistic work on transmigration of the souls, by Rabbi Chaim Vital, with a commentary by Rabbi Meir Eisenstadt. In 1682, Rabbi Yeshayah Horowitz prohibited the sale and distribution of the book, "because of the inherent danger to the [spiritual outlook of the] community." Rabbi Grunhut vowed to abide by the decree of the Frankfurt rabbinate. Rabbi Grunhut also wrote the *sefer Migdol David*, a commentary on *Bereishis* (Frankfurt, 1702). Rabbi Yeshayah was later appointed to head the rabbinate of Posen.

Rabbi Yosef Shmuel, the Mesores Hashas

The next Chief Rabbi of Frankfurt was Rabbi Yosef Shmuel of Cracow. His work *Mesores Hashas* (Frankfurt, 1721) has been of enormous benefit to anyone who has studied *Gemara*. His glosses are printed on each page of the Talmud, giving parallel sources in Talmud, Rambam, *Tur*, *Smag* and *Shulchan Aruch*.

The delegation from Frankfurt which came to Cracow to appoint Rabbi Yosef Shmuel as rabbi of their *kehillah* was so eager that they demanded a guarantee from him that he would keep his word and come to Frankfurt.

The following beautiful legend about the election of Rabbi Yosef Shmuel of Cracow is told by the Jews of Frankfurt.

Lying on his deathbed, the old Rabbi of Frankfurt summoned the *gabbaim* of the *kehillah* to his bedside.

"I am about to die," he said in a barely audible voice, "and I want to make certain that the next Rabbi of Frankfurt is qualified to lead our magnificent community. To this end I am going to present to you three difficult questions on a *sugya* in the *Gemara*. These questions have baffled me for many years, and only recently have I found a satisfactory solution to them. My suggestion is that whoever can answer these three questions is worthy to occupy the rabbinate of Frankfurt."

After the rabbi's demise, the *kehillah* selected three scholars, giving them the task of travelling the length and breadth of Europe in search of the great *talmid chacham* who would be able to solve the three questions. The delegates, travelling from town to town, finally arrived in Cracow, a city known for its outstanding scholars.

After receiving an official welcome, they were invited to participate in a *bris* that was about to take place in the home of one of the prominent members of the Cracow community. During the festive meal that followed the *bris*, the oldest son of the host, a nine-year-old boy, was called upon to deliver a *pilpul* which the local *melamed* had taught him. One can well imagine the utter surprise of the three scholars from Frankfurt when they heard this young boy ask the three questions their late rabbi had posed and, what is more, offer ingenious solutions to these problems.

"Who taught this *derashah* to this boy?" the three delegates wanted to know.

"The man who is sitting over there at the end of the table. His name is Rabbi Yosef Shmuel. He is the *shamash* of the old *shul* of Cracow. He is also a *melamed*, and this boy is one of his students."

After the meal, the committee of three immediately went to the *melamed*. They found him teaching a class of young boys.

"Forgive us for interrupting," the spokesman said, "but there is an important matter we'd like to discuss with you right now."

"I'm sorry," Rabbi Yosef Shmuel replied. "Teaching children is a holy assignment. While I'm teaching I'm not permitted to divert my time and attention to other matters. However, tonight after classes, I'll be glad to listen to you."

That evening, the men returned and proposed to him that he give up his position as *melamed* and accept the post of Chief Rabbi of Frankfurt.

"But I'm just a simple *melamed*," Rabbi Yosef Shmuel retorted. "How could I have the audacity to lead a *kehillah* as prestigious as Frankfurt?"

The three scholars now related the last words of their rabbi and urged him to accept the nomination. But Rabbi Yosef Shmuel persisted in his refusal.

Dismayed and depressed, the delegation returned home to Frankfurt. They had failed in their mission; their rabbi's wish had not been fulfilled.

Soon thereafter, Rabbi Yosef Shmuel became seriously ill, and the doctors all but gave up hope of saving him. The *melamed*, in the throes of death, turned his eyes toward Heaven.

"*Ribono Shel Olam*," he whispered. "You know very well that I did not turn down the rabbinate out of stubbornness. I am truly convinced that I am not worthy of this great honor. But if You insist that I become the Rabbi of Frankfurt, then I bow to Your Will and Wisdom."

No sooner did he end his *tefillah* than he began to feel better, and within a few days, he recovered completely. He then notified the Frankfurt community that he was willing to accept the nomination as chief rabbi of their distinguished *kehillah*.

The board of directors and all of Frankfurt Jewry, overjoyed at the good news, began to make preparations for a festive celebration for the installation of the new rabbi.

But then disaster struck.

In the Judengasse, the main street of the ghetto, the murdered body of a Christian child was found. A priest spread a rumor that the Jews had killed the Christian child in order to use his blood for baking *matzos* for their impending Passover festival. The inaugural celebration for the new rabbi was called off, and when Rabbi Yosef Shmuel arrived in Frankfurt on the appointed day, he found the community plunged in gloom and despair. He soon learned that, in the wake of the blood libel, the Frankfurt authorities had decreed a total expulsion of all the Jews, unless the Jews found the perpetrator of the murder and delivered him to the Court of Justice.

Rabbi Yosef Shmuel, in his first act as chief rabbi, promised the *kehillah* that he would personally appear in Court and point out the murderer. When the waiting period of three days had passed, the gendarmes hauled the officers of the community into court, and Rabbi Yosef Shmuel came along with them.

After the cardinal ended his summation, in which he accused the Jews of the brutal murder of the Christian child, the new rabbi asked to be heard. Addressing the court, he petitioned the chief magistrate that in the interest of justice the body of the murdered child be placed before the bench. The request was granted, and the body was brought into the courtroom.

"I am absolutely sure," the rabbi continued, "that the dead child will reveal the murderer. Let everyone present in the courtroom step forward and place his hand on the body of the victim. When the murderer touches the child's body he will be unable to remove his hand. Thus, the victim himself will identify his killer."

The cardinal, hearing the new rabbi's suggestion, broke into shrill laughter.

"Ha, ha," he sneered. "The Jews of Frankfurt imported a new rabbi from the backwoods of Poland to make fun of us! A dead man cannot testify in court, and a murder victim cannot point the finger at his killer."

The cardinal's mocking hysterics aroused the magistrate's suspicion. He decided to accede to the rabbi's suggestion. One by one, all the assembled filed past the body of the child, touching it. Nothing happened, until at last it was the cardinal's turn. When told to touch the body, he loudly protested, pounding his fist, making a spectacle of himself.

"I'm not going to be regulated by the idiotic ideas of a dim-witted Jewish rabbi," he shouted, his face flushed with anger.

But when the magistrate insisted that he place his hand on the child's body, the cardinal's face turned ashen, and breaking into a fit of uncontrollable sobs, he admitted that he had committed the murder.

The Jews of Frankfurt were elated. Thanks to the courage and wisdom of their new rabbi, a disaster had been averted.

Rabbi Yosef Shmuel served as Rabbi of Frankfurt for the next twenty-five years. Tradition has it that during these twenty-five years he reviewed the *Shas* forty-two times— while standing upright! Thereby, he literally fulfilled the command *vedibarto bam*, "speak of [the words of the Torah]," since the numeric value of *bam* amounts to forty-two.

It is, indeed, a beautiful tale, even though it is not historically accurate. It is an established fact that Rabbi Yosef Shmuel never served as *shamash* in Cracow. But in a higher sense, a legend does tell the truth, for by embellishing the events surrounding his life, the legend accurately depicts the high esteem in which Rabbi Yosef Shmuel was held by his *kehillah*. He passed away in 1703.

Chapter Five

RABBI NAFTALI KATZ AND THE GREAT FIRE

In 1704, Rabbi Naftali Katz was appointed Rabbi of Frankfurt. Rabbi Katz was the author of *Semichas Chachamim* (Frankfurt, 1704), a commentary on the Talmud that bespeaks his profound erudition.

In 1709, the following question was the subject of a great deal of animated discussion among the *Halachic* authorities of the time. "If, upon opening the carcass of a kosher slaughtered animal, no heart is found, is this animal considered fit to be eaten?"

Divergent *teshuvos* were written on the subject by the greatest *poskim* of that time. Rabbi Naftali's answer was affirmative. "Since an animal cannot live without a heart, and no heart was found, we must presume that it was misplaced. The animal is kosher."

It is interesting to note that the great Rabbi Yonasan Eybschutz, after consulting experts from the medical school of the University of Halle, ruled that such an animal is *treifah*. (*Kreisi Upleisi* 40)

During Rabbi Naftali's tenure, the community grew in scholarship and was recognized as the foremost *kehillah* in the Jewish world of that day.

Then, on January 14, 1711 (24th *Teves*), at about nine o'clock in the evening, a fire broke out in Rabbi Naftali's house. Within minutes, the flames spread to the neighboring houses, leaping from rooftop to rooftop, and before long, the entire ghetto was turned into a blazing inferno, engulfing both homes and synagogues. The wooden ghetto structures burned like tinderboxes.

Evil tongues accused the rabbi of having caused the fire. Rabbi Naftali was arrested. After explaining that the fire had been an accident, he was immediately released by the police.

Five hundred homes were destroyed in the conflagration, and eight thousand people were made homeless. Many of these unfortunates were given shelter by gracious non-Jews in the neighboring towns. Rabbi Naftali was offered hospitality by the non-Jewish master tailor Johannes Finger. Upon bidding farewell to his kindhearted host, Rabbi Naftali gave him the blessing that his descendants would never be poor. Indeed, as long as a descendant of Johannes Finger maintained a business in town, the Jews patronized his store, and thereby, Rabbi Naftali's blessing was fulfilled.

The disaster weighed so heavily on Rabbi Naftali's mind that he could no longer remain in Frankfurt. He moved to Prague, and from there he left for Eretz Yisrael. Before reaching his destination, he died en route in Constantinople, on the twenty-fourth of *Teves*, 1719, the eighth anniversary of the Great Fire.

The following authentic and very moving story is told in connection with the saintly Rabbi Naftali's grave.

Dr. Mordechai Eliash, the Israeli ambassador to Great Britain, related that his aunt Dinah Rosa Eliash is buried in

Constantinople (now Istanbul). Once, while on a visit to Istanbul, Dr. Eliash was told the following story by the secretary of the *kehillah*.

"While lying in the throes of death, Dinah Eliash called the office of the *kehillah*, requesting that the secretary of the community come to her bedside.

"'I am about to die,' the woman told the secretary, 'and I'm asking you to promise me that you will bury me alongside the grave of my ancestor Rabbi Naftali Katz.'

"The secretary had never heard of Dinah before in his life. He found her reclining in bed in a hotel room. She repeated her request to be buried alongside Rabbi Naftali Katz.

"'How can I be sure that you are indeed a descendant of this great *tzaddik*?' the secretary, whose name was Segal, replied. 'Besides, I'm only human. This cemetery has not been in use for hundreds of years, and it is completely full. How do you expect me to find a vacant plot?'

"She explained to him her lineage, reaching back to Rabbi Naftali.

"'By this time tomorrow I won't be here anymore,' she said, looking him straight in the eye. 'So please, take care of this matter, and let me know by tonight what you've accomplished.'

"Mr. Segal submitted the request to Rabbi Marcus of Istanbul.

"'One may not refuse the last wish of a dying person,' the rabbi answered. 'I'll see what I can do.'

"Toward evening, he went back to see Dinah, and she again asked for and received his promise about the burial site. She also requested that she not be transported to the cemetery in the hearse that is shared by all religions in Istanbul, but that her *aron* be borne on the shoulders of members of the *chevrah kadishah*. She then asked Mr. Segal to recite the *Neelah* prayer with her, as well as the *Viduy* and *Ata Nosein Yad* (from the *Neelah* service). Relating the incident, Mr.

Segal was moved to tears, although it happened more than twenty-three years before.

"The following day, Dinah passed away. After getting to know Dinah and witnessing her pure spirit and uprightness, Mr. Segal arranged for the Istanbul *beis din* to carry out her wishes. Besides, he ordered that the women who took care of her *taharah* immerse themselves in a *mikveh* before touching her remains and treat her body with the utmost respect.

"Meanwhile, Mr. Segal went to the old cemetery, and there, miraculously, a gravesite had appeared out of nowhere alongside the grave of the *tzaddik* Rabbi Naftali.

"'I could not believe my eyes,' Mr. Segal said. 'I had visited the grave of the *tzaddik* many times before, but I had never noticed this empty plot. We began to dig, and strangely, the earth felt soft and smooth, as though it had been prepared for the descendant of this *tzaddik*. People carried her on their shoulders to her final resting place for the entire distance of several kilometers. Rabbi Marcus gave a brief eulogy in which he said that words failed him to describe this wondrous event.'

"Since that day, the Jews of Istanbul and many visitors have been coming to pray at this grave.

"I visited the small *beis hamidrash* of Rabbi Naftali," Dr. Eliash continues. "From there we walked to the old cemetery and to the two graves.

"I was profoundly touched as I recited *Tehillim*. I stood there quietly, immersed in thought, until the sun slowly set, and we were forced to leave.

"It is interesting to note that the Belzer Rebbe was also a descendant of Rabbi Naftali Katz, but when he was in Istanbul, during his escape from the Nazis, his frail health did not allow him to travel to the grave. He sent his brother, the Bilgorayer Rav, along with two prominent *chassidim*, to implore Hashem to have compassion on the Jewish people.

"Mr. Segal, who visits the grave every *Erev Rosh Chodesh*,

was at a loss for words to describe the fervor with which the Rebbe's brother *davened* at the *kever*. The Belzer Rebbe had instructed him, 'Speak to the *tzaddik* as though you were addressing a living person. Plead with him, and beseech him to champion the cause of the remnant of Yisrael before the Heavenly Throne.'

"After copying the text of the inscription on the grave, which is in perfect condition, I returned to the city."

The *klaus* of Frankfurt was headed by Rabbi Shmuel Schotten, a renowned *lamdan* who officiated on occasion as chief rabbi. He is known for his *Kos Yeshuos* (Frankfurt, 1717), a commentary on the Talmud. Over the years, thousands of scholars attended his learned lectures.

Other eminent scholars from this era were: Rabbi Naftali Gunzburg, author of *Naftali Seva Ratzon*, a commentary on the *Chumash* (Amsterdam, 1705); Rabbi Nassan, author of *Shikchas Haleket* (Amsterdam, 1700); Rabbi Moshe Frankfurter, author of *Zeh Yenachameinu* (Amsterdam, 1712); Rabbi Yosef Kaschmann, author of *Noheg Katzon Yosef* (Hanau, 1718); Rabbi Akiva Frankfurter II, author of *Sefer Haohel Olam*, a commentary on *Kesuvos* (Frankfurt, 1714).

As soon as the community recovered from the shock of the Great Fire, the foundations for the new *shul* were laid. Two *shuls* were built; the smaller one was completed first. After the *shuls* and the homes were rebuilt, the *kehillah* chose a new rabbi. The post was filled by Rabbi Abraham Brodi, formerly the Rabbi of Raudnitz, *rosh yeshivah* of Prague and Rabbi of Metz. Young scholars flocked to hear his Talmudic lectures, so that almost all Talmudic students of his time were his disciples at one time or another. He wrote *Eshel Avraham* (Frankfurt, 1747), *chiddushim* on five tractates of the Talmud. He died in 1727.

Rabbi Yaakov Hakohen Poppers was elected as his successor. Before coming to Frankfurt, he had been the Rabbi of

Koblenz. He was one of the few rabbis of Frankfurt who wrote *teshuvos*. His collection of *teshuvos*, entitled *Shev Yaakov* (Frankfurt, 1742), gained wide acceptance. He was known as a fierce fighter against anything that was even vaguely connected with the false *mashiach* Shabsai Tzvi. This placed him at loggerheads with the acclaimed and brilliant Rabbi Moshe Chaim Luzzatto, the author of the *Mesillas Yesharim*. While today, the author of *Mesillas Yesharim* is recognized as a saintly personality, and his books are held in the highest esteem, during his lifetime many people looked askance at him and even suspected him of harboring Sabbatean sympathies, which was, of course, not true.

Once, on a visit to Frankfurt, Rabbi Moshe Chaim Luzzatto quite innocently paid a courtesy call on Rabbi Yaakov Poppers. Rabbi Poppers immediately questioned him about his beliefs and chided him for things he disapproved of. He made him sign a statement pledging "on pain of excommunication, not to teach to anyone in the world, whoever or wherever he may be, the knowledge of Kabbalah, either orally or from a book, not even the writings of the Arizal or the *Zohar*, much less the things that I myself dreamed up."

Rabbi Yaakov Poppers died in 1740.

Another Frankfurt *lamdan* of great distinction was Rabbi Moshe Kann, son-in-law of the magnate Reb Shimshon Wertheimer of Vienna. Rabbi Kann was *rosh yeshivah* of the Frankfurt *klaus* (comparable to today's *kollel*).

Chapter Six

THE PNEI YEHOSHUA AND HIS SUCCESSORS

The second half of the eighteenth century was a period of great upheaval for the Frankfurt *kehillah*. Growth came to the crowded streets of the Judengasse, which seemed to be miraculously able to hold more and more dwelling places. The larger and more prosperous community continued to suffer from disputes and dissent.

Rabbi Yaakov Yehoshua Falk, a true giant of Torah scholarship and author of the *Pnei Yehoshua* (Frankfurt, 1752), a commentary on the Talmud, brought great prestige to Frankfurt. His work is indispensable to the serious student, and the Pnei Yehoshua's insights are cited in the lectures of every present-day *rosh yeshivah*.

Rabbi Yaakov Yehoshua Falk was born in Cracow in 1680. His grandfather was the author of *Meginei Shlomo* (Amsterdam, 1715). As the son-in-law of Reb Shlomo Landau, one of the wealthy communal leaders of Lemberg, he became the *rosh yeshivah* in that city and, as he put it, "lived in happiness and contentment, surrounded by friends and students who obeyed His directives."

But a serious accident brought a sudden end to his happiness. A gunpowder storehouse exploded, destroying the entire neighborhood and turning his house into a heap of rubble. Thirty-six Jews were killed in the disaster, including his wife, his little daughter and his mother-in-law. A heavy beam fell on Rabbi Yaakov Yehoshua, pinning him down and almost crushing him. He thought that "his house had become his grave." He vowed that, if he would be saved, "he would devote himself entirely to the study of Torah and would not leave the four walls of the *beis midrash*." The rescue workers found him and extracted him from his wedged-in position.

After totally immersing himself in Torah study, he successively became the Rabbi of Tarli, Zarew and Liska, and in 1718, he was appointed to the prestigious post of Chief Rabbi of Lemberg. At that time, the Sabbatean influence was making inroads into Poland, gaining many adherents. Rabbi Yaakov Yehoshua, recognizing the danger, fulminated against the heresy, pronouncing a *cherem* on its followers. He subsequently became the Rabbi of Berlin, and from there he went to Metz to fill the position formerly held by the most respected Talmudist of that day, Rabbi Yaakov Reischer, author of the famous *Shvus Yaakov* (Halle, 1709).

In 1741, the Pnei Yehoshua assumed the chief rabbinate of Frankfurt. The Jewish world at that time was split into two opposing camps. The controversy was sparked by the accusations of Rabbi Yaakov Emden against Rabbi Yonasan Eybschutz, the Chief Rabbi of Hamburg. Rabbi Yaakov Emden, a fierce opponent of Sabbateanism, after examining an amulet written by Rabbi Yonasan Eybschutz, accused him of being a secret follower of Shabsai Tzvi's ideology. The argument exploded into a major confrontation with bitter recriminations and denunciations to the government. Soon, all of

European Jewry became involved in the acrimonious dispute. In the end, Rabbi Yonasan was cleared of all blame, and his *sefarim* rank among the most widely studied works today. They include *Kreisi Upleisi* (Altona, 1763), *Yaaros Devash* (Karlsruhe, 1779), *Urim Vetumim* (Karlsruhe, 1775) and many others.

The Frankfurt community found itself in the eye of the storm, with the Pnei Yehoshua supporting Rabbi Yaakov Emden and becoming the leading opponent of Rabbi Yonasan Eybschutz. In the aftermath of the dispute, the Pnei Yehoshua was compelled to leave Frankfurt in 1751. He moved to Worms, where he did not hold a rabbinical position. His wife, a learned woman, earned a livelihood by running a business. His opponents made life unbearable for him in Worms, forcing him to move to Offenbach, where he died in 1756.

The Pnei Yehoshua, the towering prince of the Torah whose life was marred by divisiveness and strife, was laid to rest in Frankfurt. The Noda Biyehudah, who had sided with the Pnei Yehoshua in the dispute, eulogized him as "the Light of the Exile, the famous *gaon*, pre-eminent in his generation, unique among his people . . ." The Kozhnitzer Maggid testified that *ruach hakodesh* appeared in the *beis midrash* of the Pnei Yehoshua.

A Community Reunited

After the years of rage and resentment that had polarized the Frankfurt *kehillah*, no new rabbi was chosen. Time was needed for tempers to cool and wounds to heal. Besides, the community had a rich reservoir of home-grown talent, outstanding *talmidei chachamim* who could ably tend to its needs, notably Rabbi Moshe Rapp (died in 1762), Rabbi Nassan Fulda Neumark, Rabbi Moshe Schwarzschild, Rabbi Teble Scheuer, Rabbi Michel Bing, among others. A highly

*The Frankfurt Judengasse
in the 18th century*

respected figure in the community was Dr. Asher Anshel Worms, a skilled physician and scientist who was also a noted Torah scholar. He wrote *Se'yog Latorah* (Frankfurt, 1766) on the variants in the Masoretic texts of *kri* and *ksiv*.

Gradually, living conditions in the Frankfurt ghetto began to improve. After much wrangling and heated debates, the City Council issued an edict permitting Jews to leave the ghetto even on Sundays and Christian holidays, in an emergency, to get a doctor or to mail a letter. This permission was granted, provided the Jews "go to their destination by the shortest possible route and behave in a quiet and decorous manner."

After a hiatus of three years, the *kehillah* decided to fill the vacant rabbinical position. The choice narrowed down to two candidates, Rabbi Yechezkel Landau of Prague, the illustrious author of *Noda Biyehudah*, and Rabbi Avraham Lissa. The latter was unanimously appointed to the post. Rabbi Avraham Lissa had proved his peace-loving nature by remaining neutral in the wrangling between Rabbi Yaakov Emden and Rabbi Yonasan Eybschutz. This made him the favorite in the Frankfurt community, which valued peace and reconciliation above any other consideration. Before becoming Rabbi of Lissa, Rabbi Avraham had led the communities of Yanov, Lukov and Mezritch. The Lissa community now refused to release their beloved rabbi. The Frankfurt *kehillah*, however, insisted that Rabbi Avraham keep his word, and in 1759, he assumed his new post in Frankfurt.

During these decades, Frankfurt reached undreamed-of economic prosperity. Some of the Jews of Frankfurt grew enormously wealthy, which is all the more astounding considering the wretched conditions of the Judengasse ghetto in which they were forced to live. An anonymous gentile writer, describing the Judengasse in 1792, states, "How dark and dingy this alley is! Too many houses squeezed into its narrow confines give it a black and dismal aura."

68

The writer continues, "Notwithstanding the dreary facade, most of our Jews are astute businessmen. I am not exaggerating when I say that were it not for the Jews our city

would not be the flourishing and prominent metropolis it is."

By the close of the eighteenth century, a wealthy oligarchy had emerged, whose combined income was estimated at more than six million gulden, a fabulous amount. Among the patrician families of Frankfurt are listed such names as Speyer, Schuster, Haas, Kann, Goldschmidt and Wertheimer. Curiously, Mayer Anschel Rothschild and two members of his family occupy only the eleventh place on the list of the wealthiest Jews of Frankfurt.

The house of Mayer Anschel Rothschild, the founder of the famous banking dynasty.

There can be no doubt that the Jews played a pivotal role in propelling Frankfurt into the position of one of the world's centers of banking and finance. The Jews also made a major contribution to the growth of Frankfurt in the realm of the arts and sciences.

Rabbi Avraham Lissa was revered for his brilliance, noble character, conciliatory demeanor and boundless kindheartedness. Word has it that he was a miracle worker. Even the Baal Shem Tov in faraway Podolia often spoke in glowing terms of Rabbi Avraham Lissa.

During this period, a Hebrew-speaking Christian theologian named Johann Eisenmenger, under the pretense of wanting to convert to Judaism, asked for and received instruction in the Talmud and rabbinic writings. For nineteen years he studied rabbinic literature, acquiring familiarity with *Gemara* and its commentators.

To the deep dismay of his rabbinic teachers, who considered him a promising Torah scholar, this purported lover of Torah proved to be a virulent anti-Semite in disguise. Eisenmenger wrote a book entitled *Entdecktes Judentum*, "Judaism Unmasked," which is a long anti-Semitic tirade, filled with lies and accusation about the Talmud and the Jewish people.

In 1700, through the intervention of the Frankfurt community, the Emperor ordered all the copies of the book confiscated before they had been distributed to the public. Eisenmenger sued the *kehillah* for financial damages in the amount of thirty thousand gulden, but his case was thrown out of court.

The Get of Cleve

Ironically, Rabbi Avraham Lissa, who was the epitome of kindness and harmony, became the central figure in the painful controversy surrounding the case of the *get* of Cleve. The case, which unleashed a torrent of discord and recriminations in the entire Jewish world, placed Frankfurt in the eye of the storm.

So great was the interest the case aroused that two books were written about it, *Or Hayashar* by Shimon Kopenhagen (Amsterdam, 1769) and *Or Yisrael* by Rabbi Yisrael Lipschutz (Cleve, 1770).

Briefly, this is what happened.

Yitzchak Neuburg of Mannheim married the daughter of

Yaakov Gunzenhauser from Bonn. The groom, who had shown signs of depression, disappeared on the day after the wedding, taking with him the dowry of ninety-four gold coins. He was apprehended and returned the dowry. The couple went to Cleve, where Rabbi Yisrael Lipschutz, after making a thorough investigation, issued a *get* at the request of the husband.

Ten days later, the *beis din* of Mannheim released a statement to the effect that the *get* was invalid. Inasmuch as the husband was mentally disturbed and suffering from paranoia, he was incompetent to give a *get*, and thus, the *get* had no validity.

The *beis din* of Mannheim submitted the case to Rabbi Avraham Lissa, who concurred with its decision. Deeply hurt, Rabbi Lipschutz of Cleve now presented the case to the pre-eminent *Halachic* authorities of that time, most of whom backed his position.

He received the unanimous support of such towering personalities as Rabbi Yaakov Emden, Rabbi Yosef Steinhart of Fuerth, the Shaagas Aryeh (Rabbi Aryeh Leib Gunzburg of Metz), the Merkeves Hamishneh (Rabbi Shlomo of Chelm) and that of the foremost *posek* of that day, Rabbi Yechezkel Landau of Prague, the Noda Biyehudah.

Coming to the defense of Rabbi Yisrael Lipschutz of Cleve, the Noda Biyehudah wrote, "The pious Rabbi [Abraham Lissa] and the sages of Frankfurt have allowed themselves to be duped by the Neuburg family and the influential members of the community . . ."

The Board of Directors of the Frankfurt *kehillah*, greatly incensed at what they perceived to be a slap at their revered rabbi, expressed their displeasure by enacting a decree whereby "neither the present Rabbi of Prague, nor his descendants shall ever be appointed to any post in the Frankfurt community, not even as superintendent of the sewer system. Furthermore, should any one of them pass through our community, they shall not be honored by being asked to give a public sermon or lecture."

Whether this acrimonious wrangling affected the health of the gentle and kind Rabbi Avraham Lissa is not certain. The fact is that he died in 1768, soon after the battle ended. He left an important commentary on a number of *masechtos*, entitled *Birkas Avraham* (Warsaw, 1881).

After Rabbi Avraham's death, no new chief rabbi was appointed. The day-to-day affairs of the community were ably conducted by Rabbi Nassan Maas who had held the position of *rosh yeshivah* in Frankfurt. In the divisive quarrels during the tenure of the Pnei Yehoshua and Rabbi Avraham Lissa, he remained on the sidelines, quietly teaching Torah to a circle of highly talented and brilliant young local scholars.

The Frankfurt communal record has this written about him: "He never left the tent of Torah, yet his good name is known far and wide. Above all, he made a fine name for himself as a magnanimous person who always shunned material gains."

Prominent Frankfurt personalities from this era who were close friends of Rabbi Nassan Maas were: Rabbi David Tevele Schiff, who in 1765 assumed the rabbinate of London; Rabbi Aharon Hertz Schloss, Rabbi of Offenbach; Rabbi Shlomo Posen, Rabbi of Friedberg.

The officers of the *kehillah* were in a quandary in their search for a new chief rabbi. Most of the rabbinical authorities of that time could not be considered for the position since they had opposed the Rabbi of Frankfurt in the case of the "*get* of Cleve."

The field was narrowed down to three suitable candidates, Rabbi Shmuel Schmelke Horowitz of Shiniava (later to become the famous Rebbe, Reb Schmelke of Nikolsburg), Rabbi Pinchas Horowitz of Lechovitz (Rabbi Schmelke's brother) and Rabbi Meir Barby, Rabbi of Pressburg. When the ballots were counted, Rabbi Pinchas Horowitz had garnered the majority of the votes, notwithstanding that he was known to be a *chassid*.

The Haflaah and his Successors

Rabbi Pinchas Horowitz, often called the Baal Haflaah, after the title of his best known work, was born in 1730 in Chortkov, Poland. He received his early education from his father Rabbi Tzvi, along with his two prodigious brothers, Rabbi Nachum and Rabbi Shmuel Schmelke. He soon became an ardent follower of the Rebbe Reb Ber, the Maggid of Mezritch (c.1704-1772). The Maggid was the successor to the Baal Shem Tov, the founder of *chassidus*. As a young man, Rabbi Pinchas served as Rabbi of Vitkov and Lechovitz, until he was elected as the Chief Rabbi of Frankfurt in 1772.

While he was Rabbi of Lechovitz, Rabbi Pinchas became involved in a disputed *get*. A woman who had been unchaste refused to accept a *get* from her learned and pious husband. Upon consultation, several authorities decided that the *get* be delivered to the woman by a *shaliach*. This was done. When the Noda Biyehudah heard of this *get*, he declared the divorce invalid since it violated the "ban of Rabbeinu Gershon," and he placed the husband in *cherem*. In the ensuing rabbinical debate, Rabbi Pinchas Horowitz wrote a *teshuvah* in which he respectfully but emphatically disagreed with the Noda Biyehudah. It should be remembered that it was the Noda Biyehudah who had fiercely opposed the Frankfurt rabbinate in the case of the "*get* of Cleve." It is quite possible that this *teshuvah* by Rabbi Pinchas tipped the scales in his favor to be elected as the new Chief Rabbi of Frankfurt.

Rabbi Pinchas found in Frankfurt a community with many scholars who later assumed rabbinical positions in important *kehillos*. To mention just a few: Rabbi Tevele Schiff in London, Rabbi Aharon Schloss in Offenbach, Rabbi Shmuel

Poppers in Friedberg (grandson of Rabbi Yaakov Poppers), Rabbi David Strauss in Fuerth, Rabbi Chaim Susskind Gundersheim in Koblenz and the celebrated Rabbi Yaakov Moshe David Tevele Scheuer in Mainz. A number of equally great scholars could not be persuaded to leave Frankfurt. Among these were Rabbi Yaakov Shames, who served as *rosh yeshivah*; Rabbi Mendel Lilg, who became the *rebbi* of the Chasam Sofer; Rabbi Avraham Trier, the Rabbi of the Klaus; Rabbi Mendel Bass and Rabbi Meir Schiff. These men devoted every moment of their days to the study of Torah *lishmah*, "for its own sake," without any ulterior motive. The group of eminent scholars was eclipsed by one member, a man of phenomenal greatness in both the revealed and mystical Torah. This illustrious personality was Rabbi Nassan Adler.

Rabbi Nassan Adler

Rabbi Nassan Adler, born in Frankfurt in 1742, was a descendant of Rabbi Shimon Hadarshan, author of *Yalkut Shimoni*, the first well-known Rabbi of Frankfurt.

As a young boy, he attended the lectures of the Pnei Yehoshua. However, it was Rabbi Tevele Schiff (later Chief Rabbi of London) who shaped Rabbi Nassan's independent and singular way of thinking and approach to learning. Living an ascetic life of self-denial, Rabbi Nassan attained great proficiency as a Kabbalist. Yet he was not detached from this world but delighted in helping others, dispensing advice and teaching at all hours of the day or night. He had a modest *beis midrash,* where he initiated a select group of brilliant students in his style of learning. In his *beis midrash,* the *tefillos* were said according to the *Nusach Ari,* which differed substantially from the accepted Frankfurt *nusach*.

Rabbi Nassan's most outstanding disciple was the prodigious Rabbi Moshe Sofer, better known to Jewish history as the illustrious Chasam Sofer.

Rabbi Pinchas Horowitz, the new Chief Rabbi of Frankfurt, to his chagrin, found himself at odds with his friend Rabbi Nassan Adler for the following reason.

The officers of the community were perturbed about the peculiar way of *davening* of Rabbi Nassan and his students. For example, Rabbi Nassan, who was a *kohen,* recited *Birkas Kohanim* every day. Further-

The Chasam Sofer

more, he used the Sephardic pronunciation, rather than the Ashkenazic pronunciation prevailing in Frankfurt.

When Rabbi Nassan ignored several summonses to cease and desist from these practices, he was excommunicated.

The matter was brought before the secular courts. But Rabbi Nassan was turned down, the ban was upheld, and he was forced to abide by the decree. The episode came to an end when Rabbi Nassan accepted a call to become the Rabbi of Boskovitz in Moravia (now Czechoslovakia), in 1782. Before long, he returned to Frankfurt where he again attracted a large following of dedicated young disciples. The old ban against Rabbi Nassan Adler was reinstated, but on the eleventh of *Elul,* 1800, at the urgent request of friends and adherents, the ban was lifted. Two weeks later, Rabbi Nassan Adler passed away at the age of fifty-eight. Rabbi Pinchas Horowitz delivered a moving *hesped,* in which he cried out, "We can find no consolation, for he was not a son of this earth!"

Rabbi Pinchas Horowitz and Mendelssohn

Imperceptibly at first, changes were beginning to occur in Jewish Frankfurt. The so-called Enlightenment, or *Aufklaerung* as it was called in German, was beginning to make inroads into traditional Judaism. The walls of the German ghetto slowly began to crumble, and the siren song of "emancipation, freedom and equality" was heard in the land. It was the beginning of the wild orgy of assimilation and intermarriage that culminated in the bestial horrors of the holocaust.

The person responsible for ushering in this age of falsehood and betrayal was Moses Mendelssohn (1729-1768). A child prodigy, he received a traditional Jewish education and was well versed in Torah and Talmud.

In 1743, the frail and hunchbacked Mendelssohn came to Berlin, where he met the German writer Gotthold Ephraim Lessing. Lessing introduced him into the circles of German Enlightenment.

Although he was an observant Jew, Mendelssohn made it his mission in life to bring the "blessings" of Enlightenment to the Jews of the ghetto. To this end, he translated the *Tanach* into classical German, affording the Yiddish-speaking Jews the opportunity to learn the language of the gentiles and enter their society. Mendelssohn, who is considered the father of Reform Judaism, reaped the rewards of his nefarious labor in the fact that some of his children and most of his grandchildren became Christians.

Rabbi Pinchas Horowitz, who recognized the danger inherent in Mendelssohn's translation and commentary, called *Biur*, fiercely opposed its use. On *Erev Rosh Chodesh Tammuz*, 1782, he delivered a memorable speech in which he condemned the translation as "an outrage that has been committed against Yisrael."

But inexorably, the Reform juggernaut advanced, devouring large numbers of Torah-observant Jews of Germany.

Rabbi Pinchas Horowitz was greatly loved and admired, not only by the Jewish community, but also by the gentile population of Frankfurt, which held him in high esteem for his many charitable acts. In both the years 1790 and 1792, he composed impressive hymns in honor of the coronation of the Emperors Leopold II and Francis II, which were presented to the two rulers.

He is famous for his monumental *Halachic* works, *Givas Pinchas, Haflaah, Hamakneh* and his Torah commentary, *Panim Yafos*, which follows the *chassidic* method of exegesis. Rabbi Pinchas Horowitz died in Frankfurt in 1805. He was succeeded by his son, Rabbi Tzvi Hirsch Horowitz, author of *Lachmei Todah* and *Machaneh Levi*, who died in 1817.

Chapter Seven

THE NAPOLEONIC PERIOD

The rise to power of Napoleon Bonaparte (1769-1821) brought about radical changes in Jewish life in Europe, early in the eighteenth century. After crowning himself Emperor of France, Napoleon set his sights on conquering the world. In 1805, he led his army into Germany, gaining victory at the Battle of Austerlitz in that year.

On his march through Europe, he granted civil rights to the Jews of Prussia and Austria. The Age of Reason and Enlightenment seemed to promise a life of dignity, economic advancement and social acceptance. But at what price!

To speed the process of assimilation, intermarriage and conversion, Napoleon convened a "Sanhedrin" of seventy-one members in Paris in 1807. After his victory, Napoleon established in Western Germany a "Confederacy of the Rhine" (1806), under the presidency of Karl Theodor von Dalberg, and constituted the Grand Duchy of Frankfurt (1810). In

1811, the Frankfurt ghetto was abolished, and in return for a payment of 440,000 florins, a declaration of emancipation for all citizens was proclaimed, expressly including Jews.

However, after Napoleon's defeat at Waterloo in 1815, many of the discriminatory laws were reinstated, and the Jews were astounded when they encountered violent anti-Semitism marked by the so-called "Hep-Hep" riots. (The word "hep" is an anti-Semitic slur. It is the acronym of *Hierosolyma est perdita*, Latin for "Jerusalem is lost.")

Frankfurt, too, suffered from these disorders in 1909, particularly the Rothschild family, which had begun to prosper under Napoleon. The founder of the famous dynasty was Mayer Anschel Rothschild (1743-1812), an upright, generous and Torah-observant Jew. His most successful son was Nathan Mayer, who moved to London and became one of the leading financiers in the British Empire. His brother Karl Mayer headed the Naples branch of the family banking business. Another brother, Anschel Mayer (1773-1855), remained in Frankfurt where his home was ransacked by the "Hep-Hep" rabble. He was a devoted supporter of Rabbi Samson Raphael Hirsch and made a large contribution toward the building of a new Orthodox *shul* in Frankfurt. In 1901, the Frankfurt branch of the Rothschild bank closed its doors.

During this era of transition, Rabbi Zev Wolf Heidenheim published a new edition of the *machzor* with a commentary and German translation written in Hebrew letters. The beautifully printed *machzor* bears the *haskamah* of the rabbis of Frankfurt, Rabbi Pinchas Horowitz (the Haflaah) and his son Rabbi Tzvi Hirsch Horowitz (the Machaneh Levi).

The last rabbi of the ancient *kehillah* was Rabbi Shlomo Avraham Trier (1758-1846), a *dayan* on the Frankfurt *beis din,* which was headed by Rabbi Shmuel Drach. Together with Rabbi Yitzchak Hildesheimer, he had been a delegate from Frankfurt to the Paris "Sanhedrin" that was convened by Napoleon in 1807. The *kehillah,* which had grown too weak and ineffective to attract a well-known rabbinic personality from abroad, had no choice but to make do with the services of the aged *dayan*.

Rabbi Trier tried without success to stem the rising tide of German Reform. In 1844, he published a collection of responsa from contemporary rabbis and scholars in German on the fundamental significance of circumcision in Judaism. This was how far the glory of Frankfurt had declined!

The Growth of Reform

The opening of the gates of the ghetto led to demands for equal rights for the Jews of Frankfurt. But it was not until 1824 that Frankfurt, an independent city-state, was forced by outside pressure to recognize the Jews as full-fledged citizens with equal rights. There still was some foot-dragging on the part of certain magistrates, but in 1864, full emancipation was finally achieved for Frankfurt Jews. Two years later, Frankfurt lost its status as an independent city-state, becoming part of Prussia.

Emancipation resulted in enormous prosperity for Frankfurt Jewry, and wealth led to an insatiable desire to be accepted by the non-Jewish world. In an accurate replay of the pattern described in the Torah, *"vayishman Yeshurun vayivat,* Jeshurun thus became fat and rebelled" *(Devarim* 32:15), the Jews of Germany, having prospered, abandoned the Torah of our heritage and invented a spurious "religion" named Reform.

As an initial step toward conquering the Orthodox masses, the reformers established schools and reading-groups where they taught German. As a next step they founded a school called Karlsschule (1804), named after Karl von Dalberg, the president appointed by Napoleon. This school was later renamed Philantropin, offering a decidedly secular and assimilationist curriculum. The institution became a major center for the Reform movement, and as early as 1807, modified prayers were introduced there. One of the prominent early reformers was Michael Kreuznach, editor of the monthly journal *Zion*.

In 1838, the "liberal" Jews gained the upper hand in the Frankfurt community and took control over the *kehillah*. Reform was gaining strength, threatening to engulf Frankfurt Jewry in a deluge of assimilation.

In 1819, at the instigation of the reformers, the Orthodox *cheder* schools had been closed by the police. Attendance at the Frankfurt *yeshivah*, which in 1793 still had sixty students, dwindled. In 1842, the number of Orthodox families was estimated to account for less than ten percent of the community.

The above-mentioned *teshuvah* by Rabbi Trier regarding *milah* was sparked by the demands of a Reform association, headed by Theodor Kreuznach (son of Michael), who demanded the abolition of all "Talmudic" laws—*milah*, *kashrus* and the belief in the coming of *Mashiach*. Even Leopold Zunz, one of the leaders of the "Science of Judaism" movement, was shocked at the audacity of these demands. He dismissed the sponsors, stating, "For insanity there is no cure!"

The outrages of the reformers knew no bounds. In 1845, a convention of Reform "rabbis" in Frankfurt decided, with a majority of fifteen against thirteen votes, that prayers need not be recited only in Hebrew. When a Reform "rabbi" named Leopold Stein was elected as "rabbi" of Frankfurt, Rabbi Shlomo Trier resigned in protest. The Reform movement at large was headed by Abraham Geiger (1810-1874), the ideologue and trailblazer of the movement who served as "rabbi-clergyman" in Frankfurt for several years. Ironically, this destroyer of Torah Judaism was born in Frankfurt into a family of famous rabbis.

But Reform was only one step in a downward spiral of

assimilation that ended in intermarriage and apostasy. It is estimated that more than 250,000 Jews converted in Europe in the nineteenth century. Spiritual darkness descended on the grandeur of the Frankfurt of old.

Chapter Eight

THE REVIVAL OF ORTHODOXY

Traditional Judaism in Frankfurt seemed on the road to extinction. The proud heritage of Frankfurt was trampled by the reformers, who discarded everything that was holy, erasing from their prayerbook any mention of return to Zion or *geulah*, moving the Sabbath services to Sunday, abolishing *kashrus* and *milah*, closing and stopping up the *mikveh*, not to mention the abrogation of the other *taryag mitzvos*.

Speaking about the deplorable situation, old Mrs. Gudula Rothschild, the mother of the five famous banker sons and a deeply religious woman, remarked sarcastically, "Yes, indeed! Assimilation has reached the point where '*in Frankfurt gibt es sogar schon dumme Juden*! Now we even have stupid Jews in Frankfurt!'"

Then, just as the night seemed darkest, a bright light began to flicker. A small group of eleven Orthodox Jews of Frankfurt, who had banded together to form a *chevrah shas*, decided to drop out from the Frankfurt community, which was under the absolute domination of the reformers. They courageously decided to establish a separate *kehillah*. At first, their application for government recognition was rejected,

The seal of the
Israelitische Religionsgesellschaft

but in 1851 they obtained the legal right for their congregation to secede from the general Jewish congregation, which was until then the only body recognized by the state. They named their congregation Israelitische Religionsgesellschaft (Jewish Society for Religion). The eleven men then took a daring step of calling on one of the rising stars on the Orthodox firmament to serve as rabbi of their as yet insignificant little "association."

Rabbi Samson Raphael Hirsch

The rabbi they invited to lead them was the illustrious *gaon* and Chief Rabbi of Moravia, Rabbi Samson Raphael Hirsch, whose towering personality was destined to save German Jewry from drowning in a sea of reform and assimilation and whose teachings would make a lasting impact on Torah-observant Jewry in Germany.

Rabbi Samson Raphael Hirsch was born on the twenty-fourth of the month of *Sivan*, 1808, in Hamburg. His father was a *talmid chacham* and a businessman. His grandfather, Rabbi Mendel Frankfurter, was the assistant rabbi of the

84

neighboring community of Altona. Rabbi Hirsch's mentor was Chacham Bernays, who had become Rabbi of Hamburg in 1822. Rabbi Hirsch subsequently prepared for a rabbinical career, studying under the eminent Rabbi Yaakov Ettlinger, author of the celebrated *Aruch Lener* (Altona, 1850). In 1829, he entered the University of Bonn, where he was a classmate of Abraham Geiger, who as ideologue of the Reform

Rabbi Mendel Frankfurter

movement was to become his chief antagonist. In 1830, Rabbi Hirsch received the call to be the Rabbi of Oldenburg. It was there that he came face to face with the devastating effects Reform was having on the young generation. He decided to do something about it, and wrote— under a pseudonym—*The Nineteen Letters of Ben Uziel* (Altona, 1836). The letters, which made a deep impression on German Jews, are a correspondence between a young rabbi called Naftali and his youthful friend Benjamin, who had been influenced by the ideas of Reform. In a classic German,

Rabbi Samson Raphael Hirsch, as a young man

Naftali proceeds to disprove all of Benjamin's arguments and propounds a Jewish philosophy which he termed "a scientific view of Judaism," predicated on an unquestioning belief in Torah *min hashamayim* and the binding character of the *Shulchan Aruch* (the Jewish Code of Law).

The publication of this work marked a turning point in the

history of German Jewry. It showed that Orthodox Judaism was not the sole purview of the older generation who had never studied science and culture, but that it could be embraced by someone who was thoroughly acquainted with the most advanced scientific discoveries and philosophies of the modern age.

Rabbi Samson Raphael Hirsch

In 1838, Rabbi Hirsch published *Chorev*, "Essays on Yisrael's Duties in the Diaspora." In this work, he explains the *mitzvos* of the Torah according to an ingenious system of symbolism.

In 1846, he was called to the rabbinate of Nikolsburg, one of the prestigious old *kehillos* in Europe, and soon thereafter, he received the distinction of being installed as Chief Rabbi of Moravia and Austrian Silesia. He even became a member of the Moravian Parliament.

In 1851, in the most far-reaching and noble deed of his life, he accepted the invitation of the eleven pious men of Frankfurt to head the newly founded Israelitische Religionsgesellschaft, giving up a highly respected, secure and lucrative position to be the rabbi of a small *minyan* surrounded by a community controlled by hostile reformers.

His work was blessed with success beyond his wildest dreams. Little by little, fighting every inch of the way, he infused Frankfurt with new Jewish life, organizing a *kehillah* of more than five hundred families named K'hal Adath Jeshurun. He established schools where Torah education was offered along with an up-to-date program of secular studies. A splendid *shul* was also erected with the help of a generous dona-tion by the Rothschild family.

K'hal Adath Jeshurun in Frankfurt

From 1866 until 1878, he published his monumental translation of the Pentateuch with Commentary. It has been translated into English in full and abridged versions and can be found in the libraries of most *yeshivos* and many private homes.

He fought hard for the right of the Jews to sever their connec-tion with the official reli-gious commu-nity when that community violates the principles of their religion. In 1876, a bill

in front of K'hal Adath Jeshurun on Chol Hamoed Sukkos

to this effect passed the German Parliament, and the so-called *Austrittsgemeinde* (separatist community) attained legal sta-tus. The *Austrittsgemeinde* of Frankfurt set an example emulated by many other *kehillos* throughout Germany that were dominated by reformers.

Not all leading sages agreed with Rabbi Hirsch. Notably, Rabbi Seligman Ber Bamberger of Wurzburg, a scholar of high repute, disagreed with him on the advisability of secession. Also, Rabbi Ezriel Hildesheimer, Rabbi of Eisenstadt and a leading Orthodox figure, differed with Rabbi Hirsch, but when Rabbi Hildesheimer became Rabbi of Berlin in 1869, he established a rabbinical seminary that followed Rabbi Hirsch's style in many ways.

Rabbi Samson Raphael Hirsch was a man of vision who almost single-handedly turned back the rising tide of Reform. His ideology of *"Torah im Derech Eretz,"* strict adherence to Torah law combined with secular knowledge, set a pattern for new generations of certain circles of Western European and later American Orthodox Jews who are unswervingly loyal to Hashem and His *mitzvos*, who are steeped in Torah and well-versed in secular knowledge. Rabbi Samson Raphael Hirsch died in 1888, but he lives on in his writings and his profound and original thoughts.

Rabbi Dr. Marcus Horovitz

In 1878, the main body of the Frankfurt community, recognizing that the pendulum had begun to swing in the direction of Torah observance and fearful of losing more members, chose Rabbi Dr. Mordechai (Marcus) Horovitz, a prominent Orthodox rabbi, to lead the community. Born in Ladany, Hungary, on *Purim*, 1844, Rabbi Horovitz studied at the *yeshivah* of Ujhel, the city of the *chassidic* master Rabbi Moshe Teitelbaum, author of *Yismach Moshe* and founder of the Satmar dynasty. He subsequently studied under Rabbi Dr. Ezriel Hildesheimer in Eisenstadt and received his secular education at the universities of Vienna, Budapest and Berlin.

In 1871, Rabbi Horovitz married the daughter of the renowned Rabbi Yaakov Ettlinger of Altona, the Aruch Lener. He successively held rabbinical posts in Lauenburg and Gnesen.

In 1878, he became the rabbi of the Orthodox Jews who had remained within the main community of Frankfurt. He accepted the post against the wishes of his mentor, Rabbi Ezriel Hildesheimer, who had urged him to turn down the position. Rabbi Horovitz demanded from the Reform leaders of the main community a dignified *shul* for the Orthodox Jews who remained in the community and had not seceded. A *shul* with a capacity of nine hundred seats was erected in 1882 and enlarged to hold thirteen hundred seats in 1901. The synagogue was destroyed during Kristallnacht, the "Night of the Broken Glass," in 1938.

Rabbi Mordechai Horovitz's responsa were published under the title *Mateh Levi.* He died in 1910.

Rabbi Shlomo Zalman Breuer

Rabbi Samson Raphael Hirsch was succeeded by his son-in-law, Rabbi Dr. Shlomo Zalman (Salomon) Breuer. Born in Hungary, he studied at the great *yeshivah* of Pressburg and was one of the outstanding students of the Ksav Sofer. He later attended German universities and acquired broad-based secular knowledge. He became the rabbi and *rosh yeshivah* in Papa, Hungary, in 1876 and held this post until 1888, the year he came to Frankfurt to succeed his revered father-in-law.

Rabbi Shlomo Zalman Breuer as a young man

Rabbi Salomon Breuer expanded the community founded by Rabbi

89

Samson Raphael Hirsch and strengthened the influence of the Orthodox rabbinate by establishing the "Association of Orthodox Rabbis of Germany," excluding from it rabbis who cooperated in communal work with Reform agencies. He was also one of the founding fathers of Agudath Israel, the world organization of Orthodox Jews which is guided by the pre-eminent Torah personalities and which seeks to promote the interests of Torah-observant Jewry. Realizing that without young Torah scholars the Frankfurt community had no future, Rabbi Breuer made the establishment of a *yeshivah* his first priority. In 1890, the new *yeshivah* was inaugurated, and Rabbi Shlomo Zalman Breuer's *shiurim* raised its standard of scholarship to a high level. He was its *rosh yeshivah* for thirty-six years, and during his tenure, he successfully implemented the plans Rabbi Hirsch had envisioned. In conjunction with Rabbi Pinchas Kohn, he published the *Juedische Monattschrifte* (Jewish Monthly). He wrote *Chachmah im Nachalah* and *Divrei Shlomo* (New York, 1948). He died in 1926.

Rabbi Shlomo Zalman Breuer in his later years

Rabbi Horowitz, the Unsdorfer Rav

After Rabbi Breuer's death, the *Austrittsgemeinde*, the separate Orthodox *kehillah*, was divided in its choice of a successor. There were those who wanted to continue the *Torah im Derech Eretz* approach to Judaism and appoint Rabbi Breuer's son Raphael as the new rabbi. Others favored an Eastern European rabbi who could bridge the gap between east and west and restore the former glory of Frankfurt as a bastion of Torah scholarship. After three years, the dispute was settled when Reb Yaakov Rosenheim, president of Agudath Israel World Organization, reconciled the factions and selected the young and erudite Rabbi Yosef Yonah Tzvi Halevi Horowitz as the next Chief Rabbi of Frankfurt.

A descendant of the Baal Haflaah, the erstwhile Rabbi of Frankfurt, Rabbi Yosef Yonah Tzvi Horowitz was born in Unsdorf (now Czechoslovakia) in 1892, where he studied under his grandfather, the eminent Rabbi Shmuel Rosenberg, known as the *Be'er Shmuel,* who was the *rosh yeshivah* of the celebrated *yeshivah* of Unsdorf. Rabbi Horowitz, a young man of vast Talmudic knowledge, succeeded his grandfather as *rosh yeshivah* of close to four hundred *bnei Torah* at the *yeshivah* in Unsdorf.

In 1929, Rabbi Horowitz assumed the rabbinate of K'hal Adath Jeshurun of Frankfurt and guided the community with love, dedication and consummate skill through its final years under Nazi domination. Among the many enactments he made, the most notable was the establishment of a *beis din* to which he appointed outstanding scholars of that time. These included Rabbi Yechiel Michel Schlesinger, who later founded Yeshivah Kol Torah in Jerusalem, and Rabbi Eliezer Posen, popularly known as Dayan Posen, son of Rabbi Gershon Posen, who served as *dayan* under Rabbi Salomon Breuer. In very complex cases, the advice of Rabbi Yonah Merzbach of Darmstadt was sought (later a *rosh yeshivah* in Yeshivah Kol Torah, Jerusalem). This *beis din* became the central judicial authority for all of German Jewry.

Under the Nazi regime, Rabbi Horowitz dealt with such knotty questions as whether one may stun an animal before *shechitah* by means of electric shock. He ruled against it.

During the night of the sixteenth of *Cheshvan*, the Nazis went on a rampage, burning and looting all synagogues in

Germany, in what came to be known as Kristallnacht, the "Night of the Broken Glass." It was a prelude to the holocaust. That night, Rabbi Horowitz was hauled off to the *shul* by the Nazis, who demanded that he show them where the gold and silver treasures were hidden.

By a miracle, he escaped with his life and was able to make his way to London, where he was elected president of Agudath Israel of Europe and was active in disseminating Torah. In 1950, he emigrated to the United States, where he rebuilt the Unsdorf Yeshivah, which had been destroyed by the Germans. He founded a *yeshivah* and named it K'hal Be'er Shmuel, after his grandfather.

In 1965, he moved to Eretz Yisrael, settling in Bnei Brak, where he died in 1970. Rabbi Yosef Yonah Tzvi Horowitz's sermons were published under the title *Chagvei Sela* (Bnei Brak, 1977).

Prominent Communal Leaders

Reb Yaakov Rosenheim (1870-1965) was one of the most significant communal leaders of Frankfurt Orthodox Jewry and world Orthodox Jewry in general. A native son of the city of Frankfurt, he was the publisher of *Der Israelit*, the influential weekly newspaper of Orthodox German Jewry for a period of thirty years. *Der Israelit* was edited by the well-known Rabbi Selig Schachnowitz.

Rabbi Yaakov Rosenheim

Reb Yaakov Rosenheim was an extraordinary man of unbending rectitude and passionate love for the Torah and the Jewish people. He personified the very finest and noblest qualities of German Orthodox Jewry of his time.

Der Israelit

Reb Yaakov Rosenheim took a leading part in the founding of Agudath Israel at the first *Knessiah Gedolah* in the city of Katowice, Poland, in 1912. In 1929, over a quarter of a century later, he rose to the high office of president of the Agudath Israel World Organization.

Another leader of German Orthodoxy was Rabbi Dr.

Rabbi Selig Schachnowitz

Yitzchak Breuer (1883-1946), son of Rabbi Salomon Breuer. Born in Papa, he studied at the Frankfurt *yeshivah* and practiced law in that city. A profound thinker and prolific writer, Rabbi Dr. Yitzchak Breuer was the ideologue and spokesman of Agudath Israel. He expounded on Hirschian thought in his work *Messiasspuren* (1918). He also wrote *Das Judenproblem* (1922) and *Der neue Kusari* (1934), as well as many other books.

In 1936, he emigrated to Eretz Yis-

Rabbi Dr. Yitzchak Breuer

rael and settled in Jerusalem, where he organized Poalei Agudath Israel, becoming its president.

Rabbi Nobel and Rabbi Hoffmann

The Orthodox *shul* associated with the main community of Frankfurt also retained distinguished Orthodox rabbis as its spiritual leaders. Upon the death of Rabbi Dr. Mordechai (Marcus) Horowitz, the position was filled by Rabbi Dr. Nechemiah Anton Nobel (1871-1922). He was born in Nagymed, Hungary, raised in Halberstadt and studied at the Rabbinical Seminary of Berlin under Rabbi Ezriel Hildesheimer. After serving in the rabbinates of Cologne, Koenigsberg and Hamburg, he became rabbi of the general community of Frankfurt in 1910. He was president of the General Rabbinical Union and took part in the founding of the Mizrachi movement of religious Zionism.

Rabbi Dr. Nobel was succeeded by Rabbi Dr. Jacob Hoffmann, who was also born in Hungary, in 1881, where he studied at the famous Yeshivah of Pressburg and at the University of Vienna. He held rabbinical posts in Vienna and Radovitz, and in 1922, he was chosen as chief rabbi of the general congregation of Frankfurt. He established a *yeshivah* which attracted many students. With the advent of the Hitler era, Rabbi Hoffmann became the official spokesman of Orthodox Jewry in Nazi Germany. In 1937, he was arrested by the Nazis and expelled from Germany. For several years, he served as rabbi of a New York congregation, and in 1954 he moved to Tel Aviv, where he died in 1956. Like his predecessor, Rabbi Dr. Jacob Hoffmann was a leading figure in the Mizrachi movement.

Services of the general Orthodox congregation were held in the *shul* at Boerneplatz, erected in 1882 and destroyed in Kristallnacht in 1938. The first *shul* and school building of

K'hal Adath Jeshurun was located at the corner of Schuetzenstrasse and Rechneiergrabenstrasse. The site of the new *shul* was at Friedberger Anlage, a magnificent edifice that existed from 1908 until it was burned down in 1938.

The rabbis of the separatist Orthodox community, K'hal Adath Jeshurun, played leading roles in the Agudah movement, while the rabbis of the general Orthodox community held influential posts in the Mizrachi organization.

Chapter Nine

JEWISH CONTRIBUTIONS TO THE CITY

The economic boom of Frankfurt was due to a large degree to Jewish financial and business enterprise. The comparative wealth of Frankfurt Jews is evident by the fact that, in 1900, 5,946 Jewish citizens paid 2,540,812 marks in taxes, while 34,900 non-Jews paid 3,611,815 marks. Many civic institutions, including hospitals, libraries and museums, were established by Jewish donations, especially from the Rothschild family. The liberal daily newspaper *Frankfurter Zeitung* was founded by the Jew Leopold Sonnemann, and the Frankfurt university, established in 1912, was also largely financed by Jews.

The Jewish population of Frankfurt grew steadily, but it did so at a slower rate than the non-Jewish population. In 1817, there were 3,000 Jews; in 1867, there were 7,600 Jews; in 1895, there were 19,500 Jews; and in 1930, there were 30,000 Jews.

Jewish communal institutions and organizations included two hospitals, three schools (the Philantropin of the general community and the primary and secondary schools founded by Rabbi Samson Raphael Hirsch), a *yeshivah* founded by Rabbi Salomon Breuer and two cemeteries (the old cemetery was closed in 1828). The Jewish section of the Frankfurt Municipal Library, headed before World War II by Dr. A. Freimann, had a rare collection of Hebraica and Judaica.

Many Jews of Frankfurt made outstanding contributions to the arts and sciences. Among these are the writer Ludwig Boerne, born as Loeb Baruch (1786-1837), who converted to Protestantism; the historian I.M. Jost; the artists Moritz Oppenheim and Benno Elkan; the biochemist Paul Ehrlich and the economist Franz Oppenheimer. Tragically, instead of dedicating their extraordinary talents to the advancement of Torah and Judaism, they slavishly enriched German *"Kultur."* In their attempt to curry favor with the German people, they or their descendants intermarried or converted to Christianity.

The German people showed their gratitude by murdering six million Jews in the gas chambers and crematoria of Auschwitz and Majdanek.

Chapter Ten

DESTRUCTION AND DEFIANT RENEWAL

After coming to power in Germany, Adolf Hitler immediately set out on his program of persecuting the Jews. On April 1, 1933, a boycott was declared against all Jewish firms and professionals, and on April 7, all Jewish government employees, teachers, journalists, actors and musicians were dismissed. Jewish-owned businesses were appropriated and "Aryanized." These actions were legalized by the German courts. A reign of terror began, with random arrests, torture and, in some cases, murder. The communal institutions of the Frankfurt *kehillah* expanded their services, aiding the unfortunate victims under the watchful eye of the Gestapo.

In October, 1938, all Jews of Polish origin were forced to leave the country on short notice and to abandon all their possessions. In Frankfurt, two thousand Polish Jews were shipped to Poland with only the clothes on their back.

On the night of November 10, 1938, in an ominous

overture to the holocaust, the German government incited a massive nationwide pogrom. Thirty-six Jews were killed. Thirty thousand were arrested and shipped to the Buchenwald and Dachau concentration camps, where they were tortured; many died. Three hundred *shuls* were completely destroyed, hundreds of Torah scrolls were desecrated and burned, and many Jewish cemeteries were demolished. This night, remembered as Kristallnacht ("the Night of Broken Glass"), dispelled any illusions about the fundamental humanity of German "*Kultur*" some gullible Jews still harbored.

The Germans forced the K'hal Adath Jeshurun community to combine with the general congregation to form a single community, which the Germans named Juedische Gemeinde. In 1939, this community was compelled to merge into the state-supervised Reichsvereinigung and was placed under the direct supervision of Gestapo Officer Holland.

The Holocaust

In June, 1941, the Frankfurt community had shrunk to 10,803 people who had not taken advantage of various opportunities to leave the country in the misguided belief that "the Hitler mania will pass." On October 19, 1941, these Jews were transported to Lodz, Minsk, Riga and Theresienstadt, where they perished. In September, 1943, the entire Jewish population of Frankfurt totaled 602, including half-Jews.

On the sixteenth of *Cheshvan,* 5703 (October 26, 1942), the magnificent *kehillah* of Frankfurt-am-Main ceased to exist.

Revival in America

Broken in body, stripped of all their possessions, many of

the hapless Jews of Frankfurt found a new home in America and settled in the Washington Heights section of New York. They had seen their *shuls* and *Sifrei Torah* go up in flames, but as *Chazal* say, "While the parchment was burning, the holy letters ascended upward and were not destroyed." Like the holy letters that survived the blaze, the spirit of Torah energized the hearts of these poor but undaunted refugees.

The Hand of Hashem sent the man who guided them in restoring the glory of Jewish Frankfurt that was lying in the dust: the revered Rabbi Dr. Joseph Breuer, son of Rabbi Salomon Breuer. Born in 1906 in Papa, Hungary, Rabbi Joseph Breuer succeeded his father upon his death in 1926 as *rosh yeshivah* of the Yeshivah of Frankfurt. On November 9, 1938, during the Kristallnacht riots, Rabbi Breuer was arrested by the Nazis and forced to close the *yeshivah*. It was then that he decided to emigrate to the United States.

Rabbi Dr. Joseph Breuer

A small group of immigrants from Germany had established a *minyan* in the Washington Heights section of New York City in 1938. This group invited Rabbi Breuer to become their spiritual leader, and under his inspired guidance, the modest *minyan* became the nucleus which miraculously grew into a model *kehillah* patterned and named after K'hal Adath Jeshurun, the Frankfurt *kehillah* founded by Rabbi Samson Raphael Hirsch. Emerging from the ashes of the holocaust, K'hal Adath Jeshurun has been transplanted intact to Washington Heights, a neighborhood which has earned the title of "Frankfurt on the Hudson." Under Rabbi Joseph Breuer's leadership, the community perpetuated the Hirschian ideal of *"Torah im Derech Eretz,"* observing all the distinctive traditions and *minhagim* of Frankfurt.

In the area of *minhagim*, great importance is attached to the *chazanus* of the Frankfurt *kehillah*, since it represents the archtype of western Ashkenazi tradition. It can be traced to the Maharil, Rabbi Yaakov Moelin (1365-1427), the great codifier of *minhagim,* who prohibited any deviation from the customary *niggunim*, some of which were said to have been sung by the *Leviim* in the *Beis Hamikdash*. Much attention is paid to the recitation of all *piyutim* and *selichos*, especially since some of them are linked to the history of Frankfurt.

When in the beginning of the sixteenth century *Lecha Dodi* became popular, it had to be chanted in Frankfurt for many years by an assistant *chazan* in order to stress its non-compulsory character.

In Frankfurt, every special event in the Jewish year was marked by a festive, solemn or plaintive tune, as the occasion demanded. Every *Yom Tov* had an appropriate melody of its own, thus, the *chazan's* chant served as a "musical calendar." There were different melodies for the *Kaddish* for each occasion, about twenty-five in all. A high point was reached when on *Simchas Torah* the *Jahreskaddisch* ("Year's Kaddish") recapitulated the whole range of the "musical calendar." Great stress was placed on the correct reading and cantillation (*neginah, trop*) of the Torah reading. Many inspiring *chazanus* compositions by the musical director I.M. Japhet of Frankfurt have become classics that warm the heart and bring back memories of a glorious past. The customs of *chazanus* and all other *minhagim* of Frankfurt are carefully observed in the K'hal Adath Jeshurun community of Washington Heights.

The *kehillah* prides itself on its highly acclaimed *yeshivah, beis midrash* and *kollel,* which bear the name of Rabbi Samson Raphael Hirsch. A Teachers' Seminary for Girls was named "Rivka Breuer Girls' School" after Rabbi Breuer's late wife. A beautiful *shul* is the focal point of the community. The new generation of *bnei Torah* that has grown up in Washington Heights is the pride and joy of their parents and *roshei yeshivah*. Among its many institutions, the *kehillah* has organized a system of *kashrus* supervision, whose high standards are highly respected by all groupings of Orthodox Jewry.

Rabbi Joseph Breuer, a noted Talmudic authority and Tanach scholar, wrote a translation and commentary on *Yirmiyahu* and *Yechezkel*. A jubilee volume entitled *Ateres Tzvi* was published by the community in honor of his eightieth birthday. Rav Breuer guided his *kehillah* until his death at the age of 98, in 1980.

Rabbi Shimon Schwab

In 1957, aware of the limitations imposed by his advancing years, Rabbi Breuer chose as his successor Rabbi Shimon Schwab, with whom he shared the leadership of the *kehillah* for twenty-three years.

Rabbi Shimon Schwab was born in Frankfurt in 1908 and studied at the Frankfurt Yeshivah, headed by Rabbi Salomon Breuer. In 1926, young Shimon Schwab, a budding Torah scholar, entered the Telshe Yeshivah, one of the first German *yeshivah bachurim* to learn in a Lithuanian *yeshivah*. He subsequently studied in the Mirrer Yeshivah under such towering figures as Rabbi Eliezer Yehudah (Reb Lezer Yudel) Finkel and Rabbi Yerucham Levovitz, the illustrious Mirrer *Mashgiach*.

During this period, he had personal encounters with the greatest *gedolim* of that age, including the Chafetz Chaim, the Gerrer Rebbe and others. Deeply impressed by the *yeshivah* world of Eastern Europe and the Torah giants who led it, he blended the best of the traditions of eastern and western European Jewry, developing an all-encompassing personality that later in life was to make him the trusted and much beloved leader of a cross-section of all Torah-observant groupings.

After serving as the assistant rabbi of Darmstadt, he was appointed to the rabbinate of Ichenhausen in the state of Bavaria, in 1933.

The advent of the anti-Semitism of the Hitler regime made life in Germany unbearable, and in 1936, the twenty-seven-year-old Rabbi Schwab was elected rabbi of the venerable Congregation Shearith Israel of Baltimore. Under his forceful yet mild-mannered leadership, the congregation became a vibrant center of Orthodox Jewish life. An enthusiastic activist for all Torah causes, he became an influential force in the Agudath Israel movement. In 1958, Rabbi Schwab joined the rabbinate of K'hal Adath Jeshurun of Washington Heights, together with Rabbi Joseph Breuer.

A brilliant orator, Rabbi Schwab has succeeded in enunciating Hirschian ideology and impressing it on the mind of the new generation of American-born children of the German immigrants. Under his leadership, English has taken the place of German in *shiurim, drashos* and communal announcements. He has greatly expanded the educational scope of the community, actively promoting the founding of a *Mesivta* and *Beis Yaakov*, as well as a *Beis Midrash*, a *kollel* and a teachers' seminary for girls. Rabbi Schwab's influence is not limited to the confines of his *kehillah*. His reputation as a Torah leader spans the globe, and his sagacious advice is sought by individuals and communities in the entire spectrum of Torah-true Jewry.

He is the author of a book entitled "These and Those" on Jewish education, *Beis Hasho'eivah*, perspectives and insights on the *Chumash*, and recently, *Shemesh Marpeih*, a compilation of responsa by Rabbi Samson Raphael Hirsch. He has also published *Selected Writings* and *Selected Speeches*, which are collections of some of his most celebrated essays and addresses.

To Future Generations

Five years ago, much of Rabbi Schwab's heavy workload was given over to Rabbi Zechariah Gelley, his hand-picked successor. Rabbi Gelley was born and bred in Slovakia, where he survived the holocaust as a youngster and subsequently emigrated to England. Educated at the *yeshivah* established in Sunderland by the disciples of Rabbi Eliyahu Dessler, and at the prestigious Kollel Harabbanim in Gateshead, he became a *rosh yeshivah* at an early age. He has already endeared himself to the transplanted Frankfurt *kehillah* for his personal warmth, his talents as an orator and teacher and his Torah scholarship. With wisdom and charm he continues the legacy of the glorious past of the Frankfurt-am-Main adapted to the realities of Jewish life in America.

Epilogue

Frankfurt-am-Main, the *ir ve'eim b'Yisrael*, the thousand-year-old *kehillah* that was served by such luminaries as the Shelah, the Pnei Yehoshua, the Baal Haflaah and Rabbi Samson Raphael Hirsch, has passed into oblivion. Like the great Torah centers of Babylonia, Spain, France and Eastern Europe, the Jewish Frankfurt of old has vanished. But the spirit of the Jewish Frankfurt lives on in the immortal writings of its *gedolim*. Their words are the subject of lively debate in *yeshivos* and *shtiblech* and everywhere Jews gather to study Torah or "talk in learning." And long after Germany will have decayed on the compost heap of history, the Torah that was created on its blood-soaked earth will shine brightly and illuminate the Jewish world.

Jewish Frankfurt lives on not only in the writings of its great scholars but also in the memories of the survivors, the *ud mutzal me'eish*, "the brand snatched from the burning fire." (*Zechariah* 3:2). With nostalgia they recall the dignified *tefillos* in the majestic *shul* at the Friedberger Anlage where they *davened* intently from their beloved Roedelheim Siddur and listened to the *chazan*, accompanied by the resounding voices of the choir, singing the rousing melodies that stirred the heart and inspired the soul.

But miraculously, the flame of Jewish Frankfurt has been rekindled. Transplanted into the alien soil of America, a tiny seed has taken root and grown into a mighty oak, and a semblance of that venerable Frankfurt *kehillah* continues to flourish, advancing from strength to strength. In the United States, a country where an organized *kehillah* was an unheard of phenomenon, K'hal Adath Jeshurun, under the guidance of its great rabbis, has established a *kehillah* in the classic mold, a community with its own model institutions of *kashrus*, *chinuch*, *gemilus chessed* and, of course, in the center of it all, the *beis haknesses* on Bennett Avenue.

Chazal tell us that Yaakov Avinu *lo meis*, "our Father Yaakov has not died." For as long as his children continue to live according to his traditions, he stays alive.

Indeed, the *gedolim* and simple Jews of Frankfurt have not died, for their children—far away from the old home—continue to live in the ways of their fathers and are *machazir atarah leyoshnah*, restoring the glory that once was.

Glossary

al kiddush Hashem: to sanctify the Name
aron: ark
avodah: service
bachurim: youths
Beis Din: Rabbinical court
beis haknesses: house of prayer
beis hamidrash: study hall
Beis Hamikdash: Holy Temple in Jerusalem
bris: circumcision
chassid: adherent to *Chassidus*
chazan: cantor
cheder: Elementary Torah School

cherem: excommunication
chevrah kadishah: burial society
chiddushim: analyses
chinuch: training
daven: pray
dayan: rabbinical judge
derashah: sermon
gabbai: synagogue president
gaon: Talmudic genius
gedolim: great ones
get: bill of Jewish divorce
hesped: eulogy
geulah: redemption
kashrus: state of being kosher

kehillah: community
kever: grave
kohein: hereditary priest
lamdan: Talmudic specialist
machzor: prayer book for high holy days and festivals
Mashiach: the Messiah
melamed: teacher
meshumad: apostate
mikveh: ritual bath
milah: circumcision
minyan: quorum of ten
mitzvah: Torah commandment
nusach: version
pilpul: involved Torah presentation
piyutim: poetic liturgy
posek: Halachic authority
rav: rabbi
rosh yeshivah: dean
ruach hakodesh: divine inspiration

sefarim: books
shamash: beadle
shechitah: ritual slaughter
shiurim: lectures
shul: synagogue
shtiblech: chassidic synagogues
siddur: prayer book
taharah: purification
talleisim: prayer shawls
talmid: student
talmid chacham: Torah scholar
tefillah: prayer
Tehillim: book of Psalms
teshuvah: respondum
treifah: unkosher
tzaddik: righteous person
tzedakah: charity
Viduy: declaration of transgressions; confession
yeshivah: Torah school
Yom Tov: festival